CRISIS LEADERSHIP

CRISIS LEADERSHIP

How to lead in times of crisis, threat and uncertainty

BY TIM JOHNSON

Bloomsbury Business

An imprint of Bloomsbury Publishing Plc

B L O O M S B U R Y
LONDON · OXFORD · NEW YORK · NEW DELHI · SYDNEY

Bloomsbury Business

An imprint of Bloomsbury Publishing Plc

50 Bedford Square	1385 Broadway
London	New York
WC1B 3DP	NY 10018
UK	USA

www.bloomsbury.com

BLOOMSBURY and the Diana logo are trademarks of Bloomsbury Publishing Plc

First published 2018

British Library Cataloguing-in-Publication Data
A catalogue record for this book is available from the British Library.

ISBN: HB: 978-1-4729-4282-1
ePDF: 978-1-4729-4283-8
ePub: 978-1-4729-4284-5

Library of Congress Cataloging-in-Publication Data
A catalog record for this book is available from the Library of Congress.

Cover design by Nick Castle
Cover image © Getty Images

Typeset by Deanta Global Publishing Services, Chennai, India
Printed and bound in Great Britain

To find out more about our authors and books visit www.bloomsbury.com.
Here you will find extracts, author interviews, details of forthcoming events
and the option to sign up for our newsletters.

To Henry, to Freddie. And, to Alexandra.

CONTENTS

INTRODUCTION

It has become so terribly fashionable today to talk about *turbulence*. To intone the word while bemoaning the state of the world, with a shake of the head and a furrowing of the brow, is the fashionable thing to do.

It's not surprising perhaps that this dark cloud loiters over all of us. Every day media commentators and *influencers* exacerbate this view by seeking to persuade us that humanity is, as a race, in some of sort of geopolitical, economic, sociological and scientific *last-chance saloon*.

Those who occupy the left and those on the right of the political spectrum don't just gently exchange the blame for 'society's' alledged woes, they hurl it at each other with a violent passion worthy of two tennis players slugging the ball at each other in a grand slam final.

Any semblance of an objective diagnosis as to what is *symptom* and what is *cause* to some of the challenges we face is so often either forgotten or filed as *too hard* to explore or explain.

There is, of course, no doubt that a deep gulf divides the world's monotheistic religions. Nor is there any doubt that the so-called global *elite* is having its knuckles wrapped by a disenfranchised majority who feel their needs have been overlooked by those who have gained from *globalization*.

There is a dark restlessness in the world which I too find uncomfortable.

Yet, despite all of this, I personally remain, at one level, very positive. There are many periods of history which have been downright more turbulent than this. We don't need to hunt too far in the past to find them.

The reality is that for all the structural challenges that our society faces, we enjoy, in general terms, a level of health and wealth that 100 years ago would have been unimaginable. Plus, life is unutterably rich. We can travel to any point of the planet, communicate with anyone, anywhere in the world in nanoseconds and have access to a limitless supply of *content*, be that for information or for fun.

However, at another level, I know from my work as a crisis management adviser all too well the risks that this environment brings to corporations, public sector bodies, charities and other groups of well-meaning people.

This restless *macro* picture brings changes in society's expectation of these organizations at, in relative terms, lightning speed. It also brings a heightened risk of violent physical threat from a resurgent form of brutal, urban terrorism. And, the otherworldly technological and engineering advances which enable all of these organizations to function with such extraordinary efficiency can and do go wrong. If we push things to the limit, sometimes they will break.

The net result of this is that the leaders of those organizations have to be constantly vigilant. Any of the above threats may be realized at any moment. And they are. Often without warning.

Suddenly, leaders find themselves shepherding themselves and those with whom they work through a situation which has, at best, thrown what seem like insurmountable and immovable objects in the way of them achieving their goals. Or, worse, they threaten the very viability of the organization. And, all of this happens in the unrelenting, critical glare of the public spotlight.

This book has been written to help with this (hopefully) once-in-a-career challenge. It has been written to help leaders make the transition from leader to *crisis leader.*

How I have approached this book

I believe we live in a golden age of books for organizational leaders. From Daniel Kahneman's *Thinking, Fast and Slow*, to Sam Leith's book on rhetoric

You Talkin' to Me?, to Matthew Syed's wonderful *Black Box Thinking*, there is a wealth of material for any leader seeking to expand their field of vision and draw on disciplines from a wide range of sources to help enhance their own leadership capability.

There is though very little available which addresses the topic of crisis leadership in general terms. There are many memoirs from *crisis leaders*. And, many of them are as entertaining as they are informative. Yet, they are understandably specific to a crisis, an industry or an individual.

The purpose of this book is to give generic guidance relevant to leaders of any organization.

I begin by trying to tie down some theoretical discipline. Chapter 1 therefore looks at the concept of a crisis and offers a definition for what crisis leadership is. And, isn't. Chapter 2 builds on this by exploring what steps I believe (potential) crisis leaders should undertake in their organizations to ensure that should the worst happen, the mechanisms of response, which are required to allow effective crisis leadership to be executed, are in place. (The measures proposed also have the benefit of reducing the chances an organization will suffer a crisis in the first place.)

Chapters 3–8 follow the lifecycle of the requirements that a crisis would place on a leader. Chapter 3 looks at the challenges of commencing crisis leadership. Chapter 4 looks at decision-making and is tightly linked to Chapter 5 which explores how crisis leaders can maximize team working. Chapter 6 provides guidance on leadership in public while Chapter 7 busies itself with tips on how leaders can cope with the stress of crisis leadership by examining crisis leadership in private. Chapter 8 then examines the fraught topic of ending crisis leadership.

I conclude the book in Chapter 9 by urging crisis leaders and those who influence them to do more to ensure that they are as prepared as they can be to lead during a crisis.

A brief note on the content

My intention throughout this book has to been to keep it *grounded* and *pragmatic*. The counsel I give is based on my own experience of working with and observing crisis leaders, supplemented by the advice given by those who agreed to be interviewed for this book.

I write, of course, of oil spills, terrorism, airline crashes, cyber breaches and the like. And, I do touch briefly on challenges in particular industries. But, I do it in broad terms.

There are two reasons for that. First, where I have been involved directly in the response to a specific crisis, my clients demand discretion. I provide it. But, secondly, I have been in the 'crisis room' all too often and been shown commentary written by a crisis management expert who doesn't have first-hand experience of the actual situation and the efforts being made to respond to it. It's not helpful. Therefore I avoid any danger of slipping into the trap of doing that by referencing situations I wasn't engaged in.

It's also worth noting that:

- I draw on academic and theoretical concepts where I think they help frame the points I make or add to the advice I provide. If I have missed out concepts that I ought to have included, then my apologies for that. In a book which covers a topic so vast as leadership (in whatever form), some omissions are inevitable.

- there is, in the book, an inevitable leaning towards what I refer to as *incident-driven* crises (e.g. crashes, bangs etc.) rather than *issue-driven* crises. That being said,

- this book is not about *emergency leaders* by which I mean those leaders who coordinate the immediate interventions undertaken to save lives, stem oil spills or defend against cyber breaches. It is about the overall leadership of the organization experiencing a crisis which often sits somewhat removed from the dangerous work done by brave and talented *first responders*.

- I refer throughout to *organizations* rather than *companies* or any specific type of organization. This is intentional. The advice I provide is relevant to all. However, I concede that there is bias towards organizations operating in Western countries which have the privilege (and pain) of free markets and media.

Finally, I would like to conclude by noting that in many of the sorts of situations I reference, I recognize that people lose family members or suffer other life-changing consequences. I do examine and indeed to an extent sympathize with the challenges of crisis leaders in these situations. That is the purpose of the book. However, it is far from my intention to cast them as victims in the same vein as those people who suffer genuine loss as a result of a crisis.

Acknowledgements

I would like to extend sincere thanks to all those leaders with whom I have worked during crises and also to those with whom I haven't worked directly but who I interviewed as part of my research for this book. As a practitioner who continues to practise I won't list the crisis leaders who fall into either of these camps. Discretion requires that of me. This should, however, take away none of the sincerity of the thanks I wish to convey.

I will though directly name and thank Captain Steven Hawkins, Lord (Mervyn) King, General Stanley McChrystal and Dr Keiji Fukuda for agreeing to have long-form versions of their interviews included and which help to bring to life some of the key concepts of crisis leadership from their wealth of experience.

So too Kevin Tasker who discussed with me his many years of experience helping his clients to recover from emotional and psychological trauma; so too Dr Alan Watkins who gave me the benefit of his insight into neuroscience among many other things; Nick Pope with whom I talked about teamwork, Dr. Peter Bull with whom I discussed the art of rhetoric and, last but not least, Dr Ian Mitroff who gave up well-earned vacation time in London to share his inexhaustible enthusiasm for the discipline of crisis management. No one has studied the topic in greater detail then he has.

On a personal note, I would like to thank my researcher Helen Buckman, who slaved away so tirelessly and diligently on this project; my assistant, Sarah Rankin, who has triaged my life for nearly a decade with endless good humour and my fellow directors at the wonderful firm that is Regester Larkin who gave me time and space to write this book.

Last and so far from least I would like to thank my wife Alexandra without whose patience as I stared into laptop while all those around me were having fun and without whose kindly (but constructive) criticism of my hapless early drafts, this book, would, quite simply, never have been written.

PART ONE

1

What is a crisis? And, what is effective crisis leadership?

What makes organizations work? What makes these restless tribes of people – who together form companies, political parties, public sector bodies, campaign groups or charities – function effectively? The answer is, of course, grotesquely complex. No two organizations are the same. Even organizations which purport to be united in their pursuit of the same goal have more differences than similarities.

There is though something that all organizations need irrespective of *what* they do, *where* they do it or *how* they do it. That is, of course, leadership. And, that is why leadership and its many facets are a matter of interest bordering on obsession.

However, while organizations unendingly need leadership in its many guises, there is a scenario in which leadership is required more than in any other, and in which those who are privileged enough to call themselves leaders are tested more than in any other. That is when the organizations they lead suffer a situation that they or others would deem to be a crisis.

Yet, for all the world's obsession with leadership – an obsession which it reveals itself to have had throughout the history of humanity itself – little practical guidance exists to help leaders execute the very specific discipline that I refer to as *crisis leadership*.

This book fills that gap. The purpose of the pages which follow is to help leaders understand what is required of them if and when they find themselves facing what feels like an unfathomably complex challenge under the glaring light of unrelenting, and often woundingly critical, public scrutiny.

Before I begin, two points of clarification are necessary.

First, crisis leadership is a complex concept of many layers. It may be tempting to consider only what crisis leaders must do from the point at which the crisis begins, the part of crisis leadership that Hollywood is content to address. This book covers this period in detail.

However, to only address leadership from the moment a crisis is triggered would be negligent. It would be to exclude the depth of responsibilities that are required of leaders in advance of the moment they become aware that they are about to face the biggest test of their careers. As I will explain, the execution of effective crisis leadership requires that leaders have the appropriate resources to lean upon and skilled colleagues to help them. Without anything or anyone to lead, there is no leadership of any kind. This requires considerable work in advance of a crisis.

It would also be to miss out the breadth and depth of leadership that I know is required in a crisis. Crisis leadership is required not just of the most senior person within the organization or of the most visible. The person defending the organization's actions on our television screens, for example. In most crises, the skills of many leaders are required in order that the range of tasks that together form 'crisis leadership' can be undertaken. It is frequently too much for one person. These leaders need to simultaneously act alone and in consort with each other.

Which brings me to my second point. The focus of this book is not on those leaders who are called upon to execute *emergency* response. Those leaders who battle the blaze, clean up the oil spill, restore the systems or clean up the floods.

Much has been written to support the extraordinary work that they do. Indeed, regulation often stipulates what they have to do and how they should do it.

Rather this book is focused on those leaders who sit atop an organization. It is focused on helping those leaders who are perhaps relieved of the sometimes dangerous work undertaken by those making the emergency interventions during a crisis but who shoulder the ultimate responsibility for what happened and how the organization responded. And they must steer the organization through the long-lasting consequences a crisis can leave behind it.

So, where to start? To form a robust theoretical foundation to support the practical counsel that I give in the rest of this book, I need to answer two seemingly simple questions. What is a crisis? And what is effective crisis leadership?

What is a crisis?

The journey towards a robust definition of 'effective crisis leadership' begins with an assessment of what a 'crisis' is and, perhaps just as importantly, what it isn't. After all, if we don't know what a crisis is, we cannot know what is required to lead through one effectively.

Dissecting and defining the word 'crisis' is far from straightforward. There are fewer words we hear more often in the Western media. The media would have us believe that every organization is plunged into immediate crisis with each challenge it faces. The semantic range of 'crisis' is nothing short of Herculean when we consider that the same word can be used in newspapers, on the same day, to describe the insufferable misery of those who live in a country torn apart by civil war as well as the current status of a relationship between two 'celebrities' little recognized beyond the world of reality television.

The deployment of the word in the media is loose and imprecise. It is often designed to drive conflict between two parties, or to inject (sometimes with a ludicrousness that stretches credulity) a situation with a sense of melodrama. The desired outcome is to boost readership, not to describe a state of affairs with any great precision.

Those tempted to categorize this as another example of contemporary linguistic vandalism should resist the urge to do so. In his exploration into the word 'crisis', the renowned German historian Reinhart Koselleck explains how the meaning of the word started expanding in the seventeenth century, and has since been subject to centuries of adaptation. Its etymological heritage is Greek, which is perhaps appropriate for a word of such epic use. It is derived from the Greek verb *krinō*, which means to 'separate', 'choose', 'judge' or 'decide'. The Greeks used the concept in the fields of law, medicine and theology, with the medical usage remaining dominant until the early modern period. It meant a choice between two stark alternatives, like right and wrong or salvation and damnation.

By the nineteenth century, 'crisis' had experienced a huge semantic expansion. Koselleck points out that this expansion meant a variety of meanings were given to the concept, but with few corresponding gains in clarity or precision. This has continued to the modern day; Koselleck also recognizes how its contemporary use has been 'inflated' by the media. It is now used interchangeably with words like 'unrest' or 'conflict', or to describe vaguely disturbing moods or situations. He muses, 'the concept of crisis, which once had the power to pose unavoidable, harsh and non-negotiable alternatives, has been transformed to fit the uncertainties of whatever might be favored at a given moment' (Koselleck and Richter 2006, p. 399). It is, of course, this sheer adaptability that makes it so ripe for exploitation. The word can flex its muscles as a subject, noun or adjective with consummate ease, and at the discretion of its user. This flexibility has been used for many centuries, and I have no doubt will be for many centuries to come.[1]

Therefore, the word, or concept, 'crisis' does not provide a sound starting point to unpick what effective crisis leadership is. We must dig deeper and look at the events or situations that can be described – however loosely – as a 'crisis'.

Events, dear boy, events: Different types of crises

'Events, dear boy, events' was Harold MacMillan's apparent reply when asked by a young journalist to name his biggest fear in leading the country. The former British prime minister's retort is likely to resonate with the organizational leaders of today even more than it did six decades ago. Today's organizational leaders face innumerable threats of floods, fires, terrorism, fraud, data breaches, pandemics, crashes, spills, accidents, explosions, contaminations, blackmail, kidnapping, extortion, faults, strikes, litigation, exposes, theft and hurricanes. The list of potential threats is endless, each incorporating vastly different dynamics and all holding the potential to become a crisis. A flood inspires very different mental images to blackmail, and rightly so. As events they all deserve a place on our list, but they are all very different. So, where do we begin in trying to make sense of it all?

Nassim Taleb, the genius behind the globally best selling book, *The Black Swan: The Impact of the Highly Improbable*, begs us not to. In his idiosyncratic style, Taleb passionately urges us not to 'privilege' crisp constructs over 'less elegant objects, those with messier and less tractable structures' (Taleb 2007, p. xxx).[2]

However, Taleb, whose brilliance is unquestionable, makes a living from being provocative. He doesn't have to attend to the unseemly business of implementing effective measures to deal with existential concepts in complex organizations. Leaders don't have that luxury. When it comes to behavioural matters, they reach for models and constructs to try and make sense of things. There is simply no other way to tackle the social science that is organizational life.

Happily, in the relatively youthful and niche world of crisis management, a number of academics and expert practitioners have busied themselves with trying to make sense of the extensive, but still far from comprehensive, list of potential crises above.

Economic	Informational	Destruction of property	Human resources	Reputational	Violent behavior
Labour strikes	Major violation of customer privacy from hacking	Flooding destroys factories and/or stores	Several key executives quit to join competitor	Social media campaign against company goes viral	Outsider enters premises and kills several employees
Boycott of products	Loss of propriety and confidential information	Major fire destroys key facility	Sudden, unanticipated large turnover in work force	Media coverage that company used bribes to win contracts	Employee attacks and kills another employee
Major decline in stock price	Key patents declared invalid	Hurricane or tornado wipes out several facilities	Dozens of key employees, such as airline pilots, call in sick on the same day	Rumour spreads that a major company product is contaminated	Company executive is kidnapped
Lawsuit resulting in major fines		Aircraft crashes into major facility	Large number of key technical employees declared to lack proper visas	Reports surface of widespread sexual harassment in company	Customer stampede on busiest shopping day of the year kills customer or employee
Major decline in earnings, such as key products become obsolete		Poison, such as toxic chemical or mold spreads throughout facility	Key executive becomes mentally unfit to handle job but refuses to step down	Revelation that several company officials hired prostitutes during a conference	
Bankruptcy					
Substantial fines by government					

FIGURE 1.1 *Major types of crises faced by leaders and organizations.*

Source: Expanded, adapted and updated from Mitroff, I. (2002) 'From Crisis Management to Crisis Leadership'. In *Business: The Ultimate Resource.* Cambridge, MA: Perseus Publishing. In DuBrin, A. J. (2013), *Handbook of Research on Crisis Leadership in Organizations.* London: Edward Elgar Publishing Ltd.

American academic Ian Mitroff, who has long been regarded as the pre-eminent academic in the field, manages to group the potential crises into six categories (see Figure 1.1).

Practitioner Andrew Griffin manages to rationalize them further into four boxes (see Figure 1.2).

These models can be extremely helpful. They bring some order to the apparent complexity of it all, and that alone brings comfort. However, they do much more than merely shorten the list.

Mitroff's approach is helpful as it appears to position *functional* responsibility within the organization. On the other hand, Griffin cleverly distributes crises into four boxes, each representing critical differences in dynamics; crises that emerge from outside the organization represent different challenges to those emerging from within. Equally, conditions are profoundly different when time, the most precious commodity in a crisis, is in short supply (e.g. during an incident) compared to when a crisis emerges over a period of days, weeks or months (e.g. during an issue). I refer to Griffin's model frequently throughout the book to help give context to my observations.

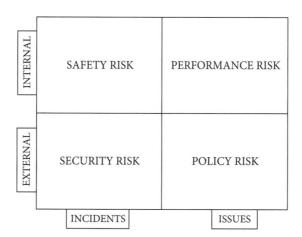

FIGURE 1.2 *Categorization of crises.*

Source: Adapted from Griffin, A. (2014), *Crisis, Issues and Reputation Management*. London: Kogan Page.

However, as both Mitroff and Griffin point out, it is important to not treat either of these models too literally. Crises don't stay obediently in their assigned boxes.

A natural disaster can begin as a safety crisis (within Griffin's typology). But, it can quickly become a policy crisis if businesses, for example, want to re-open but are forbidden from doing so by, what they might perceive to be, an over-anxious government which continues to implement civil restrictions on, say, transportation or other activities. Similarly, the level of complexity between the 'same' crises can differ enormously. Staying with the same theme, if an aircraft crashes in open fields on final approach to an airport, that is profoundly different from an aircraft disappearing in the dead of night without a trace over the Atlantic ocean. The same typology of crisis but different in so many ways.

There are though two additional 'fault lines', which run deeply through any crisis and which are critical to understanding both 'crisis' and 'crisis leadership'. These are:

1   the potential *impact* on the organization; and therefore

2   the *resources* which need to be dedicated to the response.

Both are critical. Let us take fraud as an example. Managing fraud is something multinational businesses take deadly seriously. However, while a US$100 one-off 'facilitation payment' made by an employee of a mining company in an Eastern African country is to be stamped on immediately, it is not a crisis for even a small organization, let alone a large one. Yet if that US$100 is part of a systematic attempt to defraud the organization, and is also in contravention of international legislation such as the feared US Foreign & Corrupt Practices Act (FCPA) or the UK's Anti-Bribery Act, it is a wholly different matter.

Similarly, if a hurricane grounds a charity's charter plane in a country where it provides aid, and the staff in the country have to remain in their hotel for several days, this is clearly unfortunate for those at the charity and for those to whom aid is provided. Still, it is not a crisis – not even for a small charity. It is unlikely that the charity's leadership will need to display crisis leadership or devote significant resources to it.

It is clearly impractical to treat each situation that may or may not become a crisis as separately. What is needed is a broad definition of crisis-like characteristics that take into account both of the earlier factors. It needs to be a definition that displays a great deal of precision and thoughtfulness, much more than is offered by most news organizations' subeditors as they seek to label any situation as 'a crisis', but which has enough generality to make it useful to this book.

Defining a 'crisis' with more precision

The good news is that both crisis management academics and practitioners have diligently addressed this. Collectively they have produced a huge selection of definitions. None are perfect, but none are wholly bad, and several deserve our attention if we are to get to the heart of what a crisis is, and what effective crisis leadership looks like.

American academics Erika H. James and Lynn P. Wooten, for example, define a crisis as 'any emotionally charged situation that, once it becomes public, invites negative stakeholder reaction, and thereby has the potential to threaten the financial wellbeing, reputation, survival of the firm or some portion thereof' (James and Wooten 2005, p. 142).[3] Hardly a description of a couple of feuding celebrities.

On the other hand, academic Robert R. Ulmer and his peers describe a crisis as a 'specific, unexpected, and non-routine event or series of events that create high levels of uncertainty and threaten or are perceived to threaten an organisation's high-priority goals' (Ulmer et al. 2007, p. 7).[4]

The cause of a crisis has also been taken up by that venerable organization, the British Standards Institute (BSI), which since 1901 has been a global champion of discipline and rigour. In 2014, the BSI assembled a group of crisis management professionals to revise the standards for crisis management. They resolved a crisis to be 'an abnormal and unstable situation that threatens an organization's strategic objectives, reputation or viability' (BSI 2004, p. 2).[5]

It is perhaps a very British understatement, but this definition's critical appeal is that it manages to capture the material impact of a crisis in a way that is simple, and also free of the linguistic clutter offered by some academics. Because of this, the BSI provides a perfectly sensible definition of a crisis, and is one to which I will return periodically throughout this book.

However, the definition still leaves us ill-placed to capture exactly what effective crisis leadership is. It may define what a crisis is, but it doesn't highlight the challenges a crisis leader may face, or at least not with any specificity. To help us move towards a definition of effective crisis leadership, which is the focus of the second half of this chapter, I want to lean on a definition from the academic community. This time it is from Christine Pearson and Judith Clair who, in their 1998 paper 'Reframing Crisis Management', define a crisis as:

> A low-probability, high-impact event that threatens the viability of the organization and is characterized by ambiguity of cause, effect and means of resolution, as well as by a belief that decisions must be made swiftly. (Pearson and Clair 1998, p. 60)[6]

Flaws in this definition don't require an extensive hunt. In Griffin's 'policy' typology there are crises that don't necessitate swift decisions. A mass shooting in the Berlin office of a multinational company has different decision-making dynamics to those facing people who are engaged in aggressive tax planning, which has attracted widespread and damning external scrutiny. It also fails to reference the intense external scrutiny under which leaders so often undertake crisis leadership; nor does it tackle the emotional intensity that accompanies most crisis situations. And for the largest and most stable organizations, crises often represent a threat to their strategic objectives (rather than their viability as whole). Nonetheless, unlike the BSI definition, it is powerful because it highlights the range of challenges facing a crisis leader.

What is crisis leadership?

Let's take a moment to reflect, dissect and translate Pearson and Clair's definition into plainer English. Their definition considers, by extrapolation, a crisis leader to be someone who must:

- face a challenge of critical importance that they probably haven't tackled before;

- do it without knowing the cause of the challenge, what it might do to their organization or how to fix it;

- at the same time quickly decide on a course of action.

All of this is without reference to external scrutiny or emotional impact. It is hard to overestimate this as a set of challenges for leadership. Few leaders have ever faced these sorts of circumstances, not least because, quite rightly, organizations do everything they can to avoid leaders having to work under these conditions.

So can we try and define 'crisis leadership' more neatly? Can we encapsulate a succinct description, one that is a natural extension of the 'crisis' definitions already explored?

American academic Dubrin describes a crisis leader as 'a person who leads group members through a sudden and largely unanticipated, negative and emotionally-draining circumstance' (Dubrin 2013, p. xi).[7] This definition is useful, not least because it nods towards the challenges of crisis leadership.

But we still need more. Dubrin describes what the crisis leader does, but not how they should do it. Neither does the definition provide any indication of success. A crisis leader may lead an organization through many weeks of a crisis. But, if he or she is ultimately forced to resign, they haven't been successful.

To resolve this, and to provide the rigour and foundation for the rest of the book, we must ask a number of different and specific questions:

1   What do leaders need to do to demonstrate effective crisis leadership? And, more specifically, are there competencies that are specific to leading in a crisis compared to those that are required to lead in business-as-usual circumstances?

2   How do we know if this has been done effectively? What are the markers of success?

Defining crisis leadership

The response to the latter part of the first question is, perhaps surprisingly, no. Or at least I don't think so. A recent survey in Harvard Business Review named 'flexibility to change opinions' and 'communicates openly and often' as critical leadership competencies. (Competencies meaning knowledge, skills and abilities).[8] Another, this time by management consultancy McKinsey, identified 'keeping a group organized and on task' and 'clarifies objectives rewards and consequences' as key.[9] Who would dismiss the need for any of these qualities during a crisis?

The same is true of behaviours. Passion, compassion and resilience are often touted as critical leadership behaviours – who wouldn't want these in a crisis leader?

What does change – and changes most profoundly – are the circumstances under which these competencies and behaviours need to be displayed. The extreme pressure in a crisis tests the crisis leader's leadership capabilities – and critically their ability to move between them with agility, pulling on different levers at different moments in the crisis. In doing so, it:

1   ruthlessly highlights areas in which the leader is less competent – no leader can effectively deploy all leadership competencies in equal measure; and

2 mercilessly hold up what we, in contemporary organizational life, have come to call 'overdone strengths' (or, put simply, weaknesses) for all to see and to judge.

Thus, 'crisis leadership' is better defined as:

the ability of leaders not to show *different* leadership competencies but rather to display the *same* competencies under the extreme pressures that characterize a crisis – namely uncertainty, high levels of emotion, the need for swift decision making and, at times, intolerable external scrutiny. It is this that will define success or failure.

Measures of success

In a crisis, everyone has a view on how the leadership responds. Multiple factors drive our viewpoint, ranging from political beliefs to, perhaps, personal experience of the leader in question or the organization in crisis. Our judgements are rarely impartial, and only occasionally considered.

I maintain the only sensible way to judge success is whether or not the leader keeps his or her job. Given all the complexities and idiosyncrasies of individual crises, this is simplistic, but justifiably so.

In only the smallest organizations, or in those that have a governance deficit, can leaders decide unilaterally if they are to keep their jobs in a crisis. In every other case, that decision rests with the Board, or a group of people taking a similar role. In the event of a crisis, the Board, acting in the interests of all stakeholders, forms its view with two guiding principles:

1 **Was the organizational leadership responsible, or *perceived* to be responsible, for the situation in which the organization finds itself?**
   If so, the leader must go immediately, before any crisis leadership can be executed.

2 **Given the circumstances, has the organizational leadership responded effectively?** This does not always mean restoring the status quo in the shortest time possible. As we will see in Chapter 8 this would not be always desirable, even if it were possible.

Using this as a guide to success, or at least crisis leadership efficacy, won't be without controversy. However, if a situation didn't involve controversy then it probably wasn't a crisis in the first place, and in the absence of a better measure, I will retain this one for now.

Conclusion

The principal aim of this opening chapter has been to bring some rigour to a topic that desperately needs it. It has also been to provide a solid foundation for the chapters that follow. However, in our hunt for rigour we have also identified many reasons for optimism for any leader who may have considered leading in a crisis daunting. Most notably, this is that crises don't demand a certain *type* of leader. The 'great man' theories that dominated leadership thinking when management theory emerged in the 1900s can remain consigned to history. The leadership competencies required for successful crisis leadership are the same as those required for successful leadership in daily organizational life. It is just that the circumstances are, and sometimes profoundly, different. To that extent it is perhaps an extreme example of *situational leadership*. If leaders can learn to demonstrate their leadership abilities under these circumstances, then there is no reason why they can't execute effective crisis leadership. The rest of this book sets out to help crisis leaders do precisely that.

2

Giving ourselves a fighting chance of succeeding

I hope very much that Chapter 1 left you positive and optimistic about your ability to execute crisis leadership should you be called upon to do so. However, it's now time to come down to earth with a reasonable bump.

While I don't believe the behaviours associated with high-performance leadership are fundamentally different to those needed to perform effective *crisis* leadership, that does not mean leaders can put their feet on the desk, put their hands behind their heads and wait for the next crisis. On the contrary, there is much leaders must do to ensure that they themselves and their organizations are in the best possible position so that they are able to deploy those leadership behaviours should the worst happen.

It is these preparatory activities that I address in this chapter.

Three critical preparatory activities

I have already made much of the general 'challenges' that a crisis brings that prevent leaders from demonstrating their leadership abilities just at the very moment they need them the most. And I will continue to do so. But what, specifically, are those 'challenges'? If we are to meet them, then we need to know what they are.

To answer that question, I am once again going to return to the BSI. For the BSI, these challenges are referred to as 'amplification factors' (BSI 2014, p. 15).[1] They are:

a the tempo of a crisis

b the critical need for timely decisions

c the complexity of the problems being faced

d the severity of those problems

e a prevailing atmosphere of uncertainty and anxiety.

There is much to praise about these 'factors'. They are not perhaps comprehensive, but they are a fine starting point in identifying the headwinds that leaders will face as they try and demonstrate their high-performance leadership skills in a crisis. It is for that reason that I refer to these factors throughout the book. However, for all that there is to praise about them, they remain startlingly abstract and, out of context, somewhat dry.

To bring to life the impact they can have on crisis leaders, I want to turn to Timothy Geitner, president of the Reserve Bank of New York and ultimately US Treasury Secretary at the time of the financial crisis which rocked the global markets in 2008, the after-effects of which the world continues to grapple with today. In his fascinating memoir of the period, *Stress Test: Reflections on Financial Crises*, he describes what it is like to be a crisis leader in the following disturbing terms:

The overwhelming burden of responsibility combined with the paralyzing risk of catastrophic failure; the frustration about the stuff out of your control; the uncertainty about what would help; the knowledge that even good decisions might turn out badly; the pain and guilt of neglecting your family; the loneliness and the numbness. (Geithner 2015, p. 200)[2]

Clearly, most crisis leaders do not grapple with decisions that, if made poorly, can plunge the world into an economic abyss from which it might take decades to recover. However, few people have an entire career's worth of experience in responding to crises to call upon (which Mr Geithner did). Nor do they have the full force of the US government to help provide and implement solutions (which he also had). So stress, like beauty, is in the eye of the beholder.

For me, Mr Geithner's description rings true of the way so many crisis leaders I have worked with have felt at the lowest moments of their response in a crisis. Not always of such epic geopolitical and historic proportions perhaps, but crises in which people's lives, health and livelihoods are at stake. More than anything though, it acts as a reminder as to just how wrong-headed the declaration that so many organizational leaders make when asked how they themselves and their organization would cope if faced with a crisis – which is 'we'd muddle through'.

FIGURE 2.1 *Giving yourself a chance of succeeding.*

Maybe they would. But how effectively would they *muddle through*? Frankly, they owe themselves and their followers more than that. This means that they need to prepare themselves and their organization. But how?

There is an endless number of steps that any leader can take to leave themselves in the best possible position to tackle the 'amplification' factors should they occur. Leaders' time and attention, however, is not endless. Therefore, I advise leaders to focus on just three steps (see Figure 2.1):

1   challenge their own bias towards optimism;

2   cultivate a 'crisis-ready' culture in their organization (which is built upon the most pertinent elements of what is known as a *Just Culture, High Reliability Culture* and *Normal Accident Theory*); and

3   prepare the organization – and its community of leaders – to respond rapidly in the event of a crisis.

This chapter explores each of these steps in some detail. And, I address each of them in chronological order. Each is a journey in its own right, each presents its own challenges and each requires tenacity, diligence and commitment. However, none of these steps is distinct or separate from the others. They are mutually rereinforcing and work as a sum of the individual parts to reduce the unfavourable effects of the amplification factors. I begin by addressing the most personal of the challenges for most leaders: the need to challenge their own bias towards optimism.

1 Challenge your own bias towards optimism

Trying to keep track of the words written on leadership is a fool's errand. Academics, retired businesspeople, soldiers, politicians and journalists scribble constantly to meet the seemingly insatiable desire to know what lies at the heart of effective leadership. It is the modern equivalent of medieval alchemy, but finding a definitive answer is as futile as turning lead into gold. American author Robert J. Allio has it right: it's a moving target. As organizations change, so too do their leadership requirements.[3]

However, a notable thread running through much of the leadership literature is that *optimistic* leaders make more effective leaders. Warren Bennis, one of the world's most influential thinkers on leadership agrees, reflecting how 'every exemplary leader that I have met has what seems to be an unwarranted degree of optimism – and that helps generate the energy and commitment necessary to achieve results' (Bennis 1999, p. 5).[4]

This is perhaps no great surprise. The Canadian anthropologist Lionel Tiger considers optimism to be one of humankind's most defining and adaptive characteristics, and even goes as far as to credit it for our evolution.[5] Without it, it would seem, the human race may reach the beginning of the end.

It should certainly be no surprise that it can be found in abundance among leaders. Leadership has its perks, undoubtedly. However, the daily grind of leadership is one of mixing an ever-changing cocktail of wit, charm, guile, strong-arming and subterfuge to surmount the many obstacles erected by the people and processes that make up organizational life. Without a predilection for optimism, madness would surely follow.

However, a surfeit of optimism can infuse leadership with a dangerous sugar rush. Typically referred to as 'optimism bias', this 'it-will-be-all-right' defence mechanism that we call on, consciously and subconsciously, on innumerable occasions every day, can lead to a profoundly worrying sense of invulnerability.

It's a topic that Daniel Kahneman takes issue with in his enormously influential book, *Thinking, Fast and Slow*, which now sits on leaders' bookshelves the world over. He warns that optimism bias is the most significant of our cognitive biases, noting that it is 'widespread, stubborn, and costly' (Kahneman 2012, p. 257).[6] He explains that we are prone to optimistic overconfidence; that we have a tendency to exaggerate our ability to forecast the future, and we think our goals are more achievable than they really are.

The danger for (potential future) crisis leaders, who fall victim of this intoxicating sugar intake, is twofold:

1. **They leave their organizations more vulnerable to crises.** This book is primarily about responding to rather than avoiding crises. Yet in this chapter in particular, it would be a dereliction of duty not to highlight the steps that might be considered to have more focus on prevention than cure. And this is the first of those occasions.

For an illustration of just how powerful and insidious the creep of optimism bias can be – accompanied by its close cousin, Keynes' 'animal spirits' – we need look no further than the issue that caused Mr Geithner so much pain, the 2008 banking crisis.

The growing body of memoirs about this epochal moment in economic history depict the (now departed) heads of some of the largest banks seemingly quite baffled as to how they found themselves dangling over a cliff, with only government money as a rope to stop them falling into bankruptcy (and taking the rest of the world with them).

Yet it is, of course, incredibly clear how it happened. Banks borrow short and lend long – the whole model relies entirely on the unnervingly intangible commodity of confidence. It requires neither strategic genius nor Olympic pessimism to imagine what *might* go wrong if banks stop lending to each other. Of course, that is precisely what happened in 2008. In the years running up to 2008, banks stretched their model until it broke.

It is also worth noting briefly how quickly optimism returns. As *the Economist* sardonically notes, in its essay on financial crises, finance is not merely *prone* to crises, it's *shaped* by them.[7] Many economists believe that financial crises happen roughly every decade and the financial comment sections of the heftier national and international media are crammed full of dire warnings of the next global meltdown. A surfeit of optimism can only be kept at bay for so long, or so it would seem.

2. They act as a blocker to the implementation of adequate crisis response planning. The last twenty years has produced a slew of organizational crises that beggar belief. Had I proposed some of the oil spills, airline incidents, corporate bankruptcies or cyberattacks that we have seen over the last decade as the basis for, say, a crisis simulation exercise – the sort which is staged to rehearse how an organization would respond to a major crisis – I would have been told that they were fanciful. Such a thing 'just couldn't happen'. And yet they *did* happen.

The reality is that what can happen to a leader's organization is limited only by a leader's imagination to conceive it.

Yet study after study finds a reluctance on behalf of leaders to commit resources to crisis preparedness initiatives. A 2016 study by global management consultancy, Deloitte, entitled 'A Crisis of Confidence', found that more than 76 per cent of surveyed board members believe their companies would respond effectively in a crisis. Yet fewer than half (49 per cent) of their companies have taken steps to be truly 'crisis ready'.[8]

The cause? There is rarely one reason for anything that does or doesn't happen. But my many years of experience is in sync with Australian crisis management consultant Tony Jacques' 2011 study of the barriers to the implementation of effective crisis management procedures; a prevalence of 'it can't happen to me syndrome'.[9]

Thus, the first obstacle a leader has to overcome in ensuring that he or she is well placed to stand up to the 'amplification' factors (or avoid the need to face them altogether) is themselves. An acceptance of fallibility is the first step in the process.

While managing their own bias towards optimism is a crucial first step, it is perhaps more of an internal and personal journey. Leaders need to build on that and turn thier attention towards demonstrating a set of external, observable behaviours. And at the same time they must encourage these behaviours within their wider organization. Together this helps to cultivate a *crisis-ready* culture. And it's to that I turn next.

2 Create a crisis-ready culture

Addressing the issues of leadership and organizational behaviour is a fraught business. Both are social sciences and thus come with few hard and fast rules. Rarely are there any answers that could be deemed either right or wrong. That is, of course, what makes it vexing and fascinating in equal measure.

However, it's not enough for the leader alone to become comfortable with a sense of their own professional mortality. Leaders need to diligently but appropriately ensure that their organization has a grip on its collective optimism. To ensure that the animal spirits remain under control and that the organization commits to the necessary crisis preparedness initiatives requires the leader to cultivate what I refer to as a crisis-ready organizational culture.

What is culture and what is the impact of leadership?

Before I delve any further into this, it's necessary to briefly reflect on what we mean by 'culture'. And indeed, how leaders influence it.

Countless tomes have been written on organizational culture. It's a debate that has developed in line with the interest in organizational studies, which began in a meaningful way in the nineteenth century as the large industrial organizations and first global corporations began to take shape.

For the purposes of this debate, I am content to settle with that famously reductionist definition from Terrence Deal and Allan Kennedy, which is that culture is 'the way we do things around here' (Deal and Kennedy 1982, p. 4).[10] Such a simple definition has its critics, but few would deny it's become the de facto definition for those trying to understand or influence organizational culture.

Even fewer still would deny the pivotal influence that leaders' behaviour has on organizational culture. Edgar E. Schein, in his influential book *Organizational Culture and Leadership*, notes that leaders influence culture by what they systematically 'pay attention to, measure, and control on a regular basis'. (Interestingly he also notes that they influence it in the way they 'react to critical incidents and organizational crises'). (Schein 2004, p. 246).[11]

While I don't disagree, the dry abstraction of the comments risks diluting their impact. The stark reality is that nothing influences an organization more than the leader's observable behaviours. And, not just at iconic moments of great success (or crisis) which go on to form the basis of the 'stories', which academics Gerry Johnson and Kevan Scholes believe form part and parcel of organizational culture, or the 'heroes' that Deal and Kennedy identify as being part of it,[12] but, behaviour on an ordinary day of an ordinary week (Deal and Kennedy 1982, p. 37).[13] Followers notice every aspect of a leader's behaviour. Constantly. Organizations mimic the behaviours of its community of leaders.

Addressing these observable behaviours is therefore the starting point for the cultivation of a crisis-ready culture, and this is where the influence of a Just Culture, High Reliability Organizations (HROs) and Normal Accident Theory (NAT) are so informative.

Proportionate risk is necessary

However, before I address that in detail, I'd like to make two points:

- **I am not advocating that organizations become quivering wrecks scared of their own shadow.** Innovation and *appropriate* risk taking is not just important for the organization, it is utterly essential. I am merely advocating that adventurism which results as an outcome of optimism is *proportionate*.

- **Modifying or refining organizational culture requires exquisite judgement, constant observation and regular modification.** As any leader knows, creating cultural and behavioural change is vexing and utterly inconsistent. There are occasions when a seemingly innocuous email or flippant remark made at an internal meeting can send a ripple across the organization with tangible results. Its barely noticeable but, like a yacht which is just slightly off course, the incremental behavioural changes it brings over an extended period means the organization ends up far away from its intended destination. On other occasions, leaders feel that they have signed off the most imaginative and impactful internal change programme the organizational world has ever encountered. But, the desired behavioural changes refuse to manifest themselves. The organization refuses to budge even an inch. That is, of course, why so many such initiatives fail and why incremental changes over an extended period of time are typically required. Most leaders, even those of small organizations, feel like they are steering a supertanker rather than a capricious yacht. But, even supertankers with precision GPS systems take a long time to turn.

With that in mind, let's examine the observable behaviours I believe so important to cultivating the crisis-ready culture. And, it involves stealing first from the central tenet of what has become known as 'Just Culture'.

Being 'Just'

Many years ago I was providing media training for a senior executive of a global corporation. (Being a competent media spokesperson is one of the key skills for a crisis leader. I address it in Chapter 6.) The very jocular gentleman in question was the head of engineering. The nature of the organization's business meant that any engineering lapse had the potential to kill hundreds, if not thousands, of people.

Over coffee I asked him how he slept at night given the sheer number of things that could go wrong, given the complexities of the operations he oversaw and the potential impact that any error, even a small one, could have.

His response was that, for him, it was relatively straightforward. He said errors could be fixed. Problems, mistakes even, were entirely manageable as long as the culture that existed in his team was such that they felt comfortable to voice their concerns, no matter how trivial they appeared to be. Dangers arose if they felt they couldn't speak up. At that point, manageable errors can become catastrophes. The bottom line, said my client, is: 'My team need to feel like they can call me, or their supervisor, at any time of the day or night to discuss anything that might be troubling them. That, ironically, is how I sleep.'

In a nutshell, my client had described what is referred to as a 'just culture'. That is to say a culture which doesn't punish people if they make mistakes which, given their level of training and experience, may be expected. The outcome of this is that people feel empowered to voice concerns.

The opposite is identified by Robert B. Whittingham as a blame culture, which 'over-emphasizes individual blame for human error at the expense of correcting defective systems'. He goes on to observe that such organizations have a number of characteristics in common, they tend to be secretive and lack openness cultivating an atmosphere where errors are 'swept under the carpet' (Whittingham 2004, p. 255).[14]

The body of literature on 'just culture' (and blame culture) has become voluminous due to the enormous impact it has had on organizations which undertake tasks of enormous complexity, including the medical sector and the airline sector. Common sense says that the astonishing safety record airlines, for example, enjoy despite the astounding risks they unendingly navigate simply by *being airlines* means this is surely a desirable cultural trait. (Crisis leaders have much to learn from the cockpit. It's a place we will return to in Chapter 3.)

What leaders must ask is, do they themselves encourage those who report to them to share their concerns? Or, are they still too caught up in the optimism of it all to hear concerns. Or, do they lean on fear, however unintentionally, to get things done and, in doing so, stifle the signals that might alert them to (potential) crises? And, what about the other leaders around them? How do they behave?

Answering these questions requires an abundance of self-confidence and a bountiful supply of self-awareness. It almost certainly requires leaders to be open to feedback from those they work with most closely to determine what it's like to give them 'bad news'. The gap in how leaders *intend* to make followers feel and how they *actually* make them feel never ceases to amaze me. If, as a leader you find yourself dismissing this counsel or unwilling to seek the input of others, may I gently suggest that it is you who may need it the most.

Once leaders have attended to this, they need to reflect on the culture that pervades within their wider organization.

High Reliability Organizations (HROs) versus Normal Accident Theory (NAT): an ideological battle

The starting point for any leader wanting to initiate any organizational initiative is, to put it simply, to know *where we are now* and *where we want to get to*.

Leaders now have multiple means to call upon to help ascertain the answer to the first question. The depth of experience and the range of tools and solutions the world's management consultancies use to characterize an organization's culture are startling. This is good and serves as evidence of the enormous importance placed upon the issue by organizations. It is not necessary for me to reflect in depth on those solutions here.

What is necessary though is to consider the question of *where we want to get to*. Or, in other words, how do we want the organization to be characterized if it is one that is best suited to keeping its sugar intake in check (and mounting an effective crisis response should it be needed)?

The bad news is that, as ever in the complex waters of organizational behaviour, it depends. It depends on what the organization is trying to achieve (which depends on what it does as an organization).

The good news is that a dizzying array of options are available. To work or socialize with organizational resilience professionals and organizational behaviouralists these days is to hear them talk of 'safety cultures', 'security cultures' or their attempts to foster a commitment to 'resilience culture'. This is again profoundly positive and reflects the importance placed on culture as part of 'organisational resilience'.

In my case, I advise leaders to cultivate wherever they can the best of two schools of thought: *NAT* and *HROs*.

Let's deal with them both briefly and extract the important parts.

Normal Accident Theory

NAT was put forward by the organizational sociologist Charles Perrow in his 1984 book, *Normal Accidents*. *Normal Accident's* main and somewhat depressing premise is that accidents are inevitable in complex organizations. Perrow provides countless examples of this happening – from the infamous 1979 partial melt down of a nuclear reactor on Three Mile Island to aircraft crashes. Perrow argues that complex organizations use technology that is so 'tightly coupled and complexly interactive' that accidents are inescapable – even 'normal'. It is impossible to predict or prevent all the complex parts that could go wrong. Because of this, Perrow suggests some systems that have very high catastrophic potential should be abandoned altogether. [15]

High Reliability Organizations

The counterpoint to this is High Reliability Theory. The genesis of the theory can be found in the 1980s with a group of researchers at the University of California, Berkeley. They studied complex systems and organizations that have the potential for catastrophic failures such as nuclear-powered aircraft carriers, but that manage almost error-free performance. They endeavoured to find out what distinguished this group. How, for example, did these high-risk organizations engage in such error-free performance and what was it that made them so remarkably effective? The group of researchers discovered what they all had in common was that they pursued safety to the highest degree. They all considered it an uppermost priority. This is a logical start.

However, most useful for leaders keen to ensure that they encourage the emergence of a crisis-ready culture is the contribution made by social psychologist Karl E. Weick to this debate. He believes what differentiates *HROs* from other organizations is their capacity for *mindfulness*. That is, 'a rich awareness of discriminatory detail and a capacity for action' (Weick, Sutcliffe and Obstfeld 1999, p. 37).[16] HROs are mindful as they are sensitive to impending threats, quickly able to give meaning to the unexpected, and ultimately are able to discover and correct errors before they become a crisis.

He expands on this further in 2001, with fellow HRO pioneer Kathleen Sutcliffe. In *Managing the Unexpected: Assuring High Performance in an Age of Complexity*, Weick and Sutcliffe identify five characteristics present in HROs that help them manage uncertainty and thus create the sort of crisis-ready culture leaders should, in my view, be striving to achieve. The characteristics are split into mindful *anticipation* and mindful *containment* to create a mindful infrastructure.[17]

Mindful anticipation is a:

1 **Preoccupation with failure:** HROs embrace failure and seek out weak signals.

2 **Reluctance to simplify:** HROs value detail, resist categorizing accidents and question assumptions.

3   **Sensitivity to operations**: HROs are responsive and recognize accidents are not the result of one error.

Mindful containment is a:

4   **Commitment to resilience**: HROs identify, control and correct errors before they are able to cause damage.

5   **Deference to expertise**: HROs know when to ask for help and seek opinions of those on the frontline of the organization.

While these ideologies are mischievously pitched in opposition to each other, they are neither right nor wrong. In the world of organizational behaviour almost nothing is. Leaders should therefore extract the most useful conclusions of both.

Leaders must reflect on the characteristics Weick and Sutcliffe identify and ask if their organization displays any of the characteristics they identify as critical to organizations which achieve an 'almost error-free' performance. Again, wide but informal consultation is almost certainly necessary. From there, consideration can be made as to whether more intense diagnosis is required and/or deeper intervention which pulls on the specific levers of organizational culture.

However, they must also not forget Perrow's cloudy conclusion that accidents will happen. And, the more complex, the more tightly interactive organisations are, the greater the chances of that happening. Thus, leaders must put their full weight behind a set of initiatives which ensure that the organization can respond to a crisis.

This brings me to my third and final step that leaders must undertake to give themselves a fighting chance of succeeding should they be called upon to be a crisis leader.

3 Preparing the organization and leadership to respond rapidly

Despite the surge in interest in many aspects of 'organisational resilience', robust, research-led thinking on what makes up robust and effective crisis management remains remarkably slim. Even slimmer is the attention paid to what time-poor leaders – and thus potential future 'crisis leaders' – ought to have top of mind when considering what measures their organization should be taking to ensure that should one of Perrow's 'Normal Accidents' or, worse, one of Taleb's Black Swans emerges, they can respond.

I have attempted to fill that gap by outlining the five questions anyone in a significant leadership position should ask their organization. I have also given guidance on the answers the leader ought to find acceptable. And, the answers which indicate that action ought to be taken to improve the organization's crisis preparedness.

Does someone have overall responsibility for crisis management? And what does that mean?

Like any initiative in any organization unless someone has ownership and accountability for it, it is unlikely to serve the purpose for which it is intended. And, the same is, of course, true for crisis response plans.

This is important stuff. Too many organizations have great fragility in their systems and are operating in a disrupted and disruptive environment. Plus, organizations and their leaders now need to be seen to respond to any crisis, particularly one that is *incident-driven* with supernatural speed.

Crisis management experts used to talk of the fabled golden hour – a description stolen from the medical profession – which described the period in which the organization knew of a crisis, but the external world did not. The unyielding presence of cameras in mobile phones, and the ability to instantly share what is captured via social media, means the term 'golden hour' should be reclaimed by the medical profession. It no longer exists in this capacity. Or least not in the vast majority of cases.

The purpose of the organizational crisis preparedness planning initiatives is to help organizations respond both rapidly and effectively. This means that they need:

1   **Conception**. Often no such mechanisms exist. A situation more prevalent than many people might think.

2   **Advocacy**. This is to ensure preparedness initiatives, which are often lost in the noise of organizational life, are known about.

3   **Explanation**. This ensures the initiatives are truly understood and can be used.

4   **Adaptation**. This ensures they remain relevant and are maintained with the tenacity and ongoing commitment they deserve.

All too often confusion reigns when questions are posed about who is responsible and accountable for these tasks. On too many occasions no one is. More frequently, crisis management is understood as business continuity, disaster recovery or even crisis communication. This frequently leads to departmental conflict, which achieves nothing more than further confusion and certainly won't support a cohesive, comprehensive response to a situation which at worst threatens the viability of the organization and, at best, has the potential to threaten its strategic objectives.

As shown in Figure 2.2, 'crisis management' is a function which sits 'on top' of other resilience functions or departments. Its a capablitiy which often manifests itself in the shape of a 'Crisis Management Team' (CMT) which forms to respond to a situation of such severity that it requires decision making or coordination which is beyond the authority of those running singular resilience functions such as business continuity, for example.

```
┌─────────────────────────────────────────────────┐
│           Strategic Crisis Management            │
│                                                  │
│   • Critical decision-making                     │
│   • Long-term impacts and strategy               │
│   • Reputational, commercial and organizational  │
│     recovery                                     │
└─────────────────────────────────────────────────┘
```

Operational Response (incident-driven crises)	Functional Support (incident- and issue-driven crises)
May require:	Likely to include:
• Emergency Response	• Communications
• Incident Management	• Legal
• Technical Response	• HR
• Business Continuity	• Finance
	• Regulatory
	• Government Relations
	• Security
	• IT

FIGURE 2.2 *Strategic crisis management.*

Even where this is understood, crisis management is also often understood within the organization as being the response mechanism for one type of crisis and is thus too narrow in scope. Oil companies, for example, have to deal with country evacuations as well as oil spills.

Sadly, it is all too often the case that even if someone does have responsibility they don't entirely know what falls into the scope of the task.

Organizational leaders need to know: Who owns crisis contingency planning, if anyone, and what exactly have they been tasked to do? Any confusion in the answers is clear indication of the need for a swift intervention.

Does the organization know when to mobilize its crisis response structures?

Above I have looked at who *owns* crisis management. And, below I look briefly at what a leader should be looking for in a robust structure to enable it to respond effectively. However, this is all meaningless unless the organization knows when these structures should be invoked. What, for us, should be deemed a crisis?

This may seem like an odd and perhaps abstract proposal. But, it's neither. And there are many reasons for this.

Some organizations like to avoid the use of the word 'crisis' (preferring, at times, odd euphemisms), whereas some organizations like to assign the responsibility for 'calling a crisis' to a specific executive.

Some organizations like to be highly prescriptive and dictate in very specific terms when certain elements of the response mechanisms should be invoked. Typically, these 'escalation models' might look at criteria such as an event which:

- led to the loss of life

- had a negative impact on the environment

- had a (+/-) financial impact on the organization;

- invited negative external scrutiny (e.g. by the (traditional media) or government and/or regulators).

Absent, at times, the excruciating conversations I have found myself involved in about how many deaths constitute a crisis, such 'impact' models can use be useful. On paper. Technically, they leave little room for interpretation. However, crises don't necessarily occur in a way which allows neat interpretation of their impact against predefined criteria. And, this is increasingly the case. Not least as the nature of the risks organizations face is such that they have the potential to make crises twist and contort themselves into one or more typological boxes.

In the absence of impact-based definitions which are imposed on some industries – for example the oil industry designates oil spills from *tier one* to *tier three* – many organizations are moving to much looser definitions of a situation, which may prompt the mobilization of a crisis management structure. A crisis is something which, in the interpretation of those involved, has the potential to threaten the viability of the organization or impede it in the execution of its strategic objectives over a sustained period of time and, almost certainly, to lead to negative external scrutiny.[18]

The predilection for this more open set of criteria is highly likely to swing back towards a more definitive list. Trends in organizational life are as cyclical as they are in fashion.

The point here though is, of course, not which option or variation of the two presented is chosen. The point is, does *something* exist to guide the mobilization of the crisis response mechanism? If the leader can't get a guarantee of that, then swift intervention is required.

Is the crisis management framework fit for purpose?

Having hopefully identified the circumstances under which the crisis response mechanism might be mobilized, the next logical question is what precisely is supposed to swing into action.

In the same way that there is no 'right answer' for the escalation models, there is no 'right answer' as to what an organization's crisis response mechanisms should look like. What works for one may not work for another. However, in my experience, there are consistencies in effective crisis management structures which I think leaders should challenge their organization to have in place. These can be categorized as *characteristics* and *building blocks*. I deal with each in turn.

Characteristics

When it comes to characteristics, potential future crisis leaders should check to ensure that whatever exists within their organization is:

- **Appropriate**. The framework must be *appropriate* to the size of the organization and *appropriate* to the impact of the crises it may face. Too many crisis management plans are overcomplicated. Big organizations have the resource, but complexity slows them down. Similarly, small organizations have the flexibility, but a deficit of resources limits their response ambitions. The structure put in place must appropriately serve the organization – the organization must not serve the structure.

- **Flexible**. A cyber breach may have the same material impacts as a plane crash, but the resources required are vastly different. No organization can create separate structures for each crisis it may face, so the structure has to be flexible.

- **Scalable**. The structure must be scalable. Or, at the very least, it must provide the *foundation* for scalability. As the sort of organizational crises we have witnessed over the last ten years have shown, the limits of the impact and the resources required to mitigate them are limited only by our ability to conceive of them.

- **Sustainable**. Crises and the impact of them always continue long after the news media has lost interest. While there may be a change of intensity, a crisis management framework may still be required for a considerable period of time. The structures in place must allow for that.

The building blocks should comprise of the following:

- **Call trees for mobilization**. We live in an 'always-on' world, but humankind's critical weakness is its need to sleep. There is also a professional need to travel, and to go on a vacation. There is therefore a need to ensure information can flow up the organization in a way which is both timely and accurate. Such a call tree for moblisation requires regular testing and frequent updates.[19]

FIGURE 2.3 *Crisis management involves decisions and activity at all levels.*

- **Distribution of teams**. Crises are multilayered and fiendishly complex. There also remains a need for crises to be managed as close to the geographic impact of the crisis, should specific communities of people in a contained area have been affected. Effective crisis structures are therefore typically structured to enable organizations to approach the situation from an *operational (local)*, a *tactical* (regional) and a *strategic* (global) level as shown in Figure 2.3. In very generic terms, the strategic team is the 'Crisis Management Team' referred to earlier, whereas the tactical team is often referred to as the 'Incident Management Team' and the operational team as the 'Emergency Response Team' (or similar depending on the organization). Some organizations name them the Gold, Silver and Bronze teams respectively. Many permutations exist.

There is also a growing popularity among larger organizations to lean on the US structure for crisis response known as the 'Incident Command System' (ICS), which is shown in Figure 2.4. Again though it is a question of appropriateness. Smaller organizations clearly need to adapt their structures accordingly but without losing their ability to tackle the crises at all of the layers in which they demand attention.

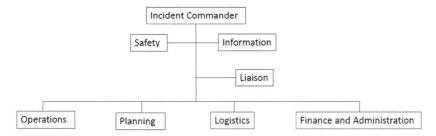

FIGURE 2.4 *The US Incident Command System (ICS).*

- **Team membership**. The question of who is on each of those teams is also an important one. Fashions change here too. Historically, each team at each layer I outlined above would have a *functional* representative so that the views and considerations of each functional lens could be given. There is much to praise about this. As I explore in Chapter 4, the nature of crises demands multiple perspectives. However, as I touch on in Chapter 5, running such teams is, for the leader, no easy feat. Thus, there is an increasing trend to shrink the team to a 'core' membership, perhaps just a leader, legal counsel and a representative of the communication function, which is supplemented by subject matter experts (SMEs) as required. Again, it's a question of organizational and indeed leadership's preference.

- **Facilities**. There is also the issue of where the teams meet and how they communicate with each other. There is, in my experience, a tendency to entirely overcomplicate discussions in this area in particular when it comes to issues of technology – a point I return to in Chapter 5. Nevertheless, teams do need space to work which is theirs alone and which enables them to meet face to face as quickly as possible. They also need a predefined dedicated conference call line, to which they all need to have swift access in the event that they are required to discuss a matter ahead of a face-to-face meeting. If all this sounds simple, that's because it is. However, it is frequently the case that organizations miss this or overcomplicate it.

- **Training and exercising**. And, much of this is, of course, for naught, unless the individuals on these teams, howsoever they are arranged, know what to and how to behave when they are mobilised. What is true for leaders is true for functional representatives. What they are being asked to do in a crisis is often not materially different to what they do on a daily basis. It's merely done *in extremis* and against the headwinds of the amplification factors. They must therefore practise. And, they must practise working with each other in these circumstances. A range of ways of doing this are available. *Desktop exercises* provide for rich discussion on how, *hypothetically*, a situation might be responded to. These are ideal for identifying gaps in contingency planning. *Simulations* provide a platform for team members to rehearse actually mobilizing a response (insofar as this is possible). Commitment to doing such exercises with regularity comes and goes. At least it does so in those organizations which have yet to experience a real crisis. In my experience, the commitment to them from those which have rarely dims.

How is the leadership organized?

I want to finish this chapter with a note on how the leadership is organized and deployed within a crisis response. It's a critical point which underpins the way in which I have structured the remainder of this book.

Figure 2.5 shows the typical structure of most large organizations. Even those which are smaller will often seek to emulate this structure within the limitations of resources they have. Overlaid on top of that structure are the specific additional 'crisis leadership' roles which typically emerge in a crisis. This begs the question as to who undertakes these roles?

Smaller organizations may have no choice but to have one person cover all of the roles or to divide the three roles among, say, two members of the leadership. That is understandable and typically manageable. Smaller

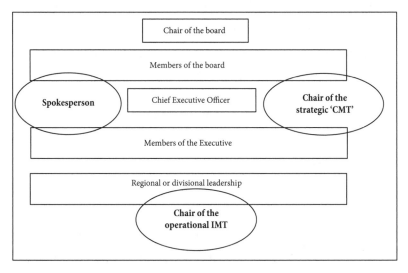

FIGURE 2.5 *Organizing crisis leadership roles.*

organizations typically have less complexity to battle, and the impact of their crisis is often less widely felt and thus attracts perhaps less external scrutiny.

However, I counsel larger organizations to consider the following:

- The **chair of the Crisis Management Team** should be a member of the executive. The role requires someone who has sufficient understanding of the organization as a whole and has the authority to make the sorts of fiendish decisions I address in Chapter 4. However, it should, wherever possible, not be the CEO. This is because the CEO has very many other roles to fill, which I have outlined below:

- **Spokesperson**. It is possible that this is a role undertaken by the CEO. However, there are many good reasons why it is also undertaken by someone else. A decision may be taken that there is a more suitable spokesperson given the nature of the situation. That is for the crisis management team (CMT) to discuss. And, I address this in more detail in Chapter 6.

- **Chair of the Incident Management Team**. This is typically a member of the regional or divisional leadership team, who has specific responsibility for the region on part of the organization and someone who must work closely with the chair of the CMT

Thus, this cadre of crisis leaders lies at the heart of an effective response to any crisis. That isn't to say that the other members of the wider community of leaders have no role. On the contrary.

The chair of the Board's role will be largely one undertaken behind the scenes. Perhaps in conjunction with other members of the board, this will be principally one of engaging with and reassuring the most senior of stakeholders, who may include government officials and, in the case of corporations the largest shareholders. It may involve mentoring or challenging the CEO. However, if the chair begins to take centre stage, it typically means that the board and shareholders are losing faith in the CEO (upon whom executive responsibility falls). Seeing the chair of the board begin to undertake television interviews during a crisis, is rarely a good sign. It's at this moment the CEO can expect a meeting to be called at short notice. And, typically at the weekend.

The role of the CEO, if not the external organizational spokesperson, is to meet with key stakeholders at times under the reassuring patronage of the chair and to ensure that the remainder of the organization continues to function as it should. Crises are akin to organizational black holes, they suck in all around them. The CEO's role is to ensure enough resources are thrown at the situation at hand. But, no more. This is a tremendously difficult balancing act. But, it's one that must be found. Finally, the CEO must also undertake rounds of internal communication to reassure the remainder of the organization that the situation is being attended to. A role so often forgotten.

The wider executive's and the wider regional or divisional leadership's role is to keep the organization moving forward.

All of this, of course, sounds terribly easy and very logical. That's because it is.

The problem is that if the leadership team has not discussed in advance how they intend to organize themselves in a crisis, they then have a habit of falling over themselves if mobilized in anger. Sometimes this is for the right reasons. In the rush to help, they hinder. Sometimes it's not for the right reasons. And, the outcome is the same even if the intention has been different.

The challenge is that it often isn't discussed in advance. The reason for that? It can be ongoing conflict among the leadership. Rubbing sores that exist is something that everyone wants to avoid.

But, in my experience, it's more typically due to the defence mechanisms provided so neatly by the optimism bias which allows leaders to leverage the 'we'd muddle through' or 'I don't have time' excuses as they whisper to themselves, 'it can't happen to me.'

And that is why I began this chapter with the counsel that I did.

Conclusion

The remainder of this book is dedicated to outlining the competencies that, primarily, the chair of the CMT is required to master (i.e. high-performance leadership in crisis conditions). That is with the exception of Chapter 6, which tackles the issue of being an organizational spokesperson. However, the counsel I give is, I hope, helpful to any member of the leadership community listed in Figure 2.5 for they will *all* have to execute 'crisis leadership' to some extent. And, of course, smaller organizations do not have the luxury of being able to allocate roles across a wider number of people. The roles listed are taken by just one person.

The advice I give though in the pages which follow assume that the leadership has adhered to the counsel I have given in this chapter and they have the resources I describe to call upon. A failure to have followed my advice will make the task of executing effective crisis leadership materially harder than it might have been.

PART TWO

INTRODUCTION

I used part one of this book to lay some important theoretical foundations that will, I hope, lead you to reflect on the concept of 'crisis leadership' in a more considered way than perhaps you might have done before.

I also invested a not inconsiderable number of words on the steps I believe leaders should take *before* a crisis occurs. This included urging leaders to battle their own bias towards optimism as well as urging them to cultivate a crisis-ready culture. The happy consequence of both of these steps being that a diligent commitment to undertaking them means an organization is less likely to find itself in a crisis in the first place. Prevention, of course, always being better than a cure.

I also outlined the steps I believe leaders should take to ensure that, should a crisis occur, the organization has the mechanisms in place to enable it to respond *rapidly* and the team structures to respond *effectively*. That, at least, is the theory.

My message is, I hope, clear: effective crisis leadership does not start at the moment the crisis occurs. It begins far in advance of that. However, no amount of pre-planning will achieve anything if, when confronted with them, the crisis leader collapses under the weight of the amplification factors I have explored in part one.

Part two is therefore dedicated to helping leaders to maximize their chance of rising to the extraordinary challenges they bring.

Consistent with the argument I have made in Chapter 1, it doesn't outline rafts of competencies that leaders should be able to master nor behaviours they need to be able to display that are wholly different from those that they require every day of the week. Rather it is dedicated to helping leaders demonstrate these competencies and display these behaviours in the crushing conditions of a crisis.

It therefore explores:

- Commencing crisis leadership; the role of the leader in those opening hours of a crisis.

- Decision-making and setting strategic direction; how leaders can cope with the intractable trade-offs that they are likely to have to make in the early 'containment' phase of a crisis.

- Running an effective team; when all eyes are upon them, how the leader gets the very best from everyone.

- Leading in public; how the leadership tackles the unenviable task of representing the organization in the media.

- Leading in private; how leaders maintain the sort of personal resilience they will need during a crisis.

- Ending the crisis and returning the organization to business as usual; how leaders know when 'the end' has come.

Let's get started.

3

Commencing crisis leadership

When leaders reflect on their careers, certain moments will stand out. If they are unfortunate to have experienced one, then one of those moments will be the point at which they found out that a crisis affecting their organization was underway.

Every discussion I have had with a leader about a crisis, as well as every speech I have heard and every memoir I have read, starts with the leader outlining where he or she was when he or she heard the news, read the tweet or received the phone call. It's a moment that becomes scarred on the leader's memory for life. And for good reason.

It is, of course, also a moment that is scarred on the memory of any 'followers' who were there at that moment the leader received the news, scouring the leader's reaction for a clue as to how they should temper their own response. That is why it is one of the moments that contribute towards the 'myths and legends', as Johnson and Scholes refer to them, that become integral to an organization's history and the topic of so many 'do you remember when' conversations.[1]

Leaders will, of course, want that moment to be remembered favourably. However, their legacy is almost certainly not likely to be at the top of their mind at the moment they received the news. Or at least it shouldn't be. What should be at the top of the leader's mind is: *'What is required of me, what is required of my organization, and how can I ensure that I use all the resources available to me, including the people around to me, to achieve that?'*

In my experience, the key to answering all of those questions – and indeed executing whatever it is that you conclude is required of you and your organization – is the need to secure the two commodities that I believe make all the difference between an effective and ineffective response to a crisis. They are:

- **Time**: It is critical that leaders set a pace that will allow them to lead the organization effectively and indeed for the organization to execute its response with diligence and efficacy. In military terms this is the 'battle rhythm'. And critical to this is the need for

- **Space:** It is vital that leaders create and use cognitive space to consider what options are available to them. As I explore in detail in Chapter 4, crises always bring trade-offs; if they didn't, there wouldn't be a crisis. Space is needed to consider these trade-offs.

Whenever I am working with a leader during a crisis, a key to success is that the leader manages the crisis, the crisis does not manage the leader. And central to that is the effective use of these vital commodities.

Incident-driven versus issues-driven crises

However, the use of them differs dramatically between an *event-* or *incident-driven* crisis and *issues-driven* crisis.

Incident-driven crises are those that so often spring to mind when you are asked to name a crisis: they include *crashes, spills, explosions* and *leaks* and typically fall into Griffin's *security* or *safety* typologies. They are mostly sudden, and occur largely without (obvious) warning. It is unlikely that the crisis leader will hear about the situation any sooner than anyone else, despite the call trees discussed in Chapter 2. In fact, there is a chance they hear about it later than some stakeholders. Photos of a major incident that happens in the smart phone era will be tweeted and posted within minutes if not seconds of it happening. No call tree works more quickly than that.

The suddenness of event-driven crises, combined with their violence, sense of violation and their instant arrival in the public domain, jolts crisis leaders into thinking they must act immediately. Clearly, and where relevant, the *emergency response* leaders have to act immediately. But, the response of the *strategic* crisis leader should be different. Rather than acting immediately, the strategic crisis leader should begin to do whatever they can to buy the time and to create the space which allows them to effectively execute their role. To put it bluntly, the challenge in an event-driven crisis is usually to slow the tempo of thought and action.

While event-driven crises occupy the media's attention immediately and for longer periods of time – with their compelling, spectacular images – an organization's strategic objectives are equally threatened by issues-driven crises.

These tend to fall into the *policy* and *performance* categories in Griffin's matrix.

They are the insidious, slow-burning crises such as incremental disruptions in technology which quickly gather pace but are not appreciated in time to stop them undermining an entire business model. Or they are an issue catalysed into being an existential threat by a change in the policy or regulatory environment which removes a key point of competitive advantage.

In an issues-driven crisis, the challenge for the crisis leader is less about the creation of *more* time and space. That is present in abundance, certainly at the outset. It is rather more about creating a sense of urgency. A missed opportunity to tackle the emerging crisis swiftly leads to a potential failure of crisis leadership.

Thus, I need to tackle both separately. And I begin with incident-driven crisis.

Incident-driven crises and emotional intelligence

Today's leaders are the Emotional Intelligent (or 'EQ') generation who were brought up on, or at least heavily influenced, by Daniel Goleman's theory that effective leaders display high levels of EQ. That is to say that they are taught the act of self-regulation or the ability to control, or redirect, disruptive impulses and moods.[2] It is something leaders practise every day, and is of tremendous benefit to any crisis leader in the hunt for time and space in a crisis. They are, to some degree, rehearsed in doing precisely what they should do when they hear about an unfolding crisis – that is to remain calm, composed and reflect very little demonstrable emotion as the first step towards securing the time and space they need for themselves and their organization.

The outcome of this is that few leaders display 'panic' in the way it is stereotypically characterized when they hear the first news of a crisis. However, what is entirely common is that leaders lurch towards coming to instantaneous conclusions which results in them issuing a rapid set of instructions. Or they become engulfed in indecision and a sort of cognitive paralysis.

Before I outline the steps I recommend a leader takes to avoid being afflicted by either of these inefficient responses, I want to outline why they occur. And to do that requires a basic understanding of how the brain works.

Basic neuroscience

The brain comprises three parts.

1 **The brainstem**. This controls our breathing and our heart rate. These are the things we do subconsciously and continuously.

2 **The prefrontal cortex (PFC)**. This manages *executive function* and differentiates humans from animals as it enables rational thought,

the ability to synthesize ideas, and to plan and to solve problems. It works with the limbic system to nuance our *emotional response* to situations.

3   **The limbic system**. This is critical to our fight-or-flight mechanism (which I explain below). The limbic system is the emotional control centre and so crucial to crisis leaders. It manages our emotions, memories and arousal by working with the thalamus (which takes information from our senses (e.g. touch and smell)), the hypothalamus (responsible for producing hormones and helping us control temperature and food intake) and the hippocampus (which converts short-term memories into long-term ones).

Within the limbic system sits something called the *amygdala*. The amygdala is two acorn-shaped bundles of nerves, and it is the emergency button in our brain, responsible for our 'fight or flight' mechanism. It is an extraordinary evolutionary tool. It is constantly scanning our environment, assessing potential threats at astonishing speed. It takes the amygdala milliseconds to process threatening information, and milliseconds for our bodies to react. The next time you hit the brake in your car instinctively to avoid an unexpected obstacle, thank your amygdala.

However, the speed and efficacy of the amygdala is both a blessing and curse. The amygdala is capable of executing what Daniel Goleman refers to as an 'emotional hijack' (Goleman 1996, p. 13).[3] When we face a fight-or-flight situation, the amygdala overrides the activity of our prefrontal cortex by releasing the stress hormone cortisol. This has an immediate physical and cognitive impact.

It sends epinephrine (adrenaline) coursing through our blood stream, which alters our physical composure and quickens our breathing to maximize our oxygen intake and deliver a surge of blood to our muscles to prepare our body to either run or fight. Or in some cases, 'play dead'.

This all matters for two reasons:

1   **It affects our ability to think**. How often, at times of high emotion, high stress, bereavement or threat, have you said the words, 'I just can't think straight'? That's because you can't. The part of the brain deployed to do so has been demoted. The cortisol reduces the levels of glucose and oxygen available to power the prefrontal cortex, which creates the sensation of 'brain fog'. The impact of this is unique to each individual, as is the speed at which that person is able to take back control by introducing rational thought to kick-start the PFC. Until control is restored, it can cause leaders to generalize and think in a linear rather that creative way. It is here that the dangers for crisis leaders emerge. They either issue an ill-considered, rapid-fire set of instructions. Or they fail to provide direction at all.

2   **It impacts our behaviour and that of those around us**. Every time we inform someone of bad news, we scan their face and body language for physical and emotional cues to gauge their reaction. Has their pallor changed? Has the speed at which they speak quickened or the pitch of their voice raised? We want to know how badly the receiver of the news believes it to be, so we can moderate our own response. In a professional context, we are also searching for any sign that blame is being laid at our door. Crisis leaders should therefore be aware of how their physical reactions send signals to those around them. This is something that Captain Steven Hawkins expands on in my interview with him which concludes this chapter.

So, what can be done about it? How can we regain control of our executive function? And, in doing so how do we secure the time and the space the crisis leader needs to commence effective crisis leadership?

Managing emotions to regain time and space

In my experience, crisis leaders should take a series of practical steps on being given news of an incident-driven crisis. The process of taking these steps will re-engage the prefrontal cortex and therefore the *executive function*, the outcome of which is the time and space critical to managing the crisis in its first stages and beyond. Specifically these steps are:

1 Resist the urge to do anything *immediately*.

2 Use (predefined), structured questions for sense-making and diagnostics.

3 Throw a communication defence around the organization.

4 Move to mobilization.

5 Ensure leadership clarity.

6 Find space to think.

I examine each in turn.

1 Resist the urge to do anything immediately

Perhaps surprisingly, it is former US President George W Bush who gifts us an excellent example of the most effective way for crisis leaders to respond on receipt of an incident-driven crisis.

At 0905 (Eastern Standard Time) on 11 September 2001, Andrew Card, the then president's chief-of-staff, entered the classroom at the Emma E Booker Elementary School in Sarasota, Florida, and told the President that a second plane had hit the World Trade Centre in New York City. The terrorist atrocity that would become known as '9/11' was underway. Thousands of critical words have been written about this historic moment. It has, of course, prompted ridicule not least because George W Bush continued to hold a copy of *The Pet Goat* – the children's book he was holding on receipt of the news – upside down. A tabloid newspaper's gift. However, I want to focus on President Bush's ability to marshal himself into doing nothing at *that moment*. He did not tear himself away from his young audience at high speed and begin barking instructions. He did nothing. He explains why he did this in a moving interview for National Geographic marking ten years since the attack.[4] The former President explains that he didn't want his reaction to do anything to increase any sense of fear in his followers – nor any sense of victory in those who were perpetrating the attack. While judgement of the strategy Mr Bush ultimately went on to take will divide opinion for centuries to come, in doing what he did, at *that moment*, President Bush did precisely what I recommend leaders should do. By not outwardly reacting, he bought himself *space* to think and *time* to react.

2 Use (predefined) structured questions for sense-making and diagnostics

Once leaders have regulated their very initial response, they must begin to make sense of what has happened. The defined concept of *sense-making* was introduced by Karl E. Weick, an American organizational theorist, to explain the process we go through to understand what is going on in a complex environment. I explore this in much greater detail in Chapter 4 when I look at decision-making in a crisis. However, I need to introduce it here as the second step for crisis leaders. And, its execution is, on paper, staggeringly simple. Crisis leaders need to ask six questions:

1 What, as far as we know, has happened?

2 When did it happen?

3 Where has it happened?

4 Who has been impacted?

5 What have we done in response so far?

6 Are there any immediate indications of *how* it has happened or *who* is responsible (in, say, the case of a cyber breach or a possible terrorist attack)?

At this point, I cannot stress enough how hard it is to do this seemingly simple task. Driven by the amygdala, every sinew in your body is propelling you to *do something* while the brain fog continues. Even in the artificial context of a crisis simulation exercise, I watch as crisis leaders get demonstrably frustrated at having to implement this step in the process. Occasionally, they simply skip it because, as they tend to concede when I review how they have approached the scenario I have given them, it's just so hard – a fact that they typically won't accept when I warn them of this in advance of starting the exercise. Throw in the amplification factors of a real crisis and it's an a enormously dangerous weak spot.

For proof of its criticality, we need look no further than the airline industry. Work undertaken by NASA in the 1970s, and outlined neatly in Cooper, Whiler Lawser's 1980 paper *Resource Management on the flight deck*, discovered that airlines were suffering fatal accidents, not necessarily through equipment failure, but because of human error when aircraft captains (many of whom were former air force pilots) were failing to engage with their crew when challenges emerged.[5] Critically, they were taking evasive action before correctly diagnosing the problems that were arising in conjunction with their colleagues. They were solving the *wrong* problem, the result of which was catastrophic. This resulted in a radical overhaul of pilot training with effective, collaborative problem diagnosis taking centre stage in flight deck instruction. Captain Hawkins, chief training pilot at British Airways, explains the powerful impact of this in his contribution to this chapter. My view on this is clear. If flight crew, responsible for the lives of hundreds of people at 35,000 feet, can take the time to run through a series of diagnostic questions, then so too can the designated crisis leader operating a few storeys from the ground.

A cautionary note does need to be sounded here. There is little chance that these questions can be answered fully in the opening moments of a crisis. The full set of trade-offs to be considered will emerge. Over time.

However, the purpose of this sense-making process is not only to work out what has happened and what should be done next. The process also stimulates the crisis leader's followers into delivering the most effective response.

In times of crisis followers, self-evidently, need leadership. The news of a crisis can cause a sudden and profound sense of loss for an organization's employees. The future that they had visualized is potentially lost in an instant.

As a result, they themselves may well be suffering from emotional hijack. The quickest way for followers to regain their composure is to observe a leader who appears to be in control. Seeing a leader calmly work through these questions is a simple but powerful way for a leader to demonstrate that control. The symbiotic relationship between the leader and follower is thus restored, and the first step towards effective resolution of the crisis and successful crisis leadership has been taken.

3 Throw a communications defence around the organization

The next action is typically part of the communication response for any organization in the event of a crisis and that is the release of a tweet, followed by a brief 'holding statement' which is put onto the organization's website. The press office is then mobilized to answer questions put to the organization by the media. Depending on the nature of the organization and its role, as well as the

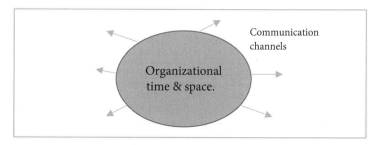

FIGURE 3.1 *Communication-led defence to provide time and space.*

nature of the crisis, helplines are established be they for customers, passengers or local community members or any other of the myriad potentially impacted stakeholders.

This is not, of course, an action for the leader to take. However, it is an action for the leader to check has been done and to appreciate more fully than, in my experience, leaders typically do. It provides a powerful channel to provide information and reassurance to people who are affected by what's happened. But, as shown in Figure 3.1, it also throws a powerful protective ring around the organization, allowing it and its leadership time and space to consider the medium-to-longer-term strategic direction that can be taken.

4 Move to mobilization

Triggering the mobilization of the crisis response teams ought, perhaps, to be the most straightforward of the steps. But, in my experience it is often one many leaders find daunting. Even for those who have been through the process of agreeing on the sort of impact-based escalation criteria I have outlined in Chapter 2, it is a challenging step.

There are, of course, times when the interpretation of those criteria is not clear cut, and therefore a moment of consideration is understandable. However, I have known more than one occasion when it is patently obvious that the broader response mechanisms need to be triggered and yet the leader has shied away from doing so. The reasons for this can, of course, vary. The brain fog of the amygdala almost certainly plays its part on some occasions. However, so too can a toxic cocktail of optimism bias and *denial* (about which I will talk in greater detail in Chapter 4), a reluctance to be seen to 'cry wolf' as well as a desire to display (what might be perceived to be) *heroic leadership*.

Because there is no one reason for the delay, there is no one solution to this surprising Achilles heel. However, I find the crisis management principles of one of the major energy company's I have worked with instructive. Based on the principle of 'prudent overreaction', it recognizes with an abundance of common sense that it's quicker and easier to stand teams down on the basis of a potential overreaction than it is to stand them up and begin the response too late. I can think of fewer more sensible mantras for crisis leaders who are poised ready to mobilize but find themselves unable, or indeed unwilling, to do so.

5 Ensure leadership clarity

In Chapter 2, I have covered the different roles that different leaders should play in a crisis. For those organizations which have the luxury of enough resources to split the various leadership roles (and are thus large and complicated enough to warrant doing so), determining swift clarity on who is running the CMT is necessary. Again, even for those organizations which have predetermined a 'duty CMT leader', a brief call between the 'Duty CMT leader' and the CEO to confirm roles is always a sensible next step as the amygdala goes to work clouding everyone's judgement. What must, at all costs, be avoided is an observable jostle for this role in the opening hours of a crisis. It wastes valuable time and disenfranchises colleagues and would certainly secure a negative legacy for those leaders interested in such matters. The issue of who is assigned to be spokesperson will also need to be dealt with, typically in conjunction with the communication team. This can come afterwards. By which I mean directly afterwards. In some crises, particularly those involving loss of life or in which there is a physical manifestation of the crisis (e.g. a crash site etc.), the demand to see and hear from an organizational representative begins almost immediately.

6 Find space to think

Finally, the crisis leader reaches his or her goal – time to reflect and space to do so.

Already a lot has been achieved, in a very short space of time. In some cases, in no more than a few minutes, the leader has been informed, has understood the very basics of the situation and has reassured followers by slowing the pace through structured questions and directing the crisis response teams to be mobilized. The leader has also, hopefully, in doing all of these things, kick-started his or her prefrontal cortex, leaving him or her cognitively more able to deal with the challenges ahead.

But, no strategic decisions have been made yet. And, nor should they have been. It's too early. Despite the (now hopefully diminishing cry of the amygdala) heavy demands on the leader to do something, the situation isn't ready yet for anything other than remedial and evasive actions, which will be happening at an emergency response or functional level. But, soon it will be, and the next key test will be to chair the first meeting of the crisis management team (assuming one exists) once the team has mobilized. And, it is now, in the brief time ahead of that meeting, either alone or with one or two close advisers, that the crisis leader can begin to prepare for that by asking the central questions that will determine the strategic response, namely: *What is required of me, what is required of my organization* and *how can I ensure that I use all the resources available to me, including the people around to me, to achieve that?*

The answers to those questions will come through skilled decision-making and team working, which the leader will be expected to execute and oversee in the coming days and weeks. Both are activities leaders do all day every day. But, executing them at times of crisis is an enormous challenge. And, I examine both the activities in detail in Chapters 4 and 5.

Checklists: Giving them a chance

Before I conclude this chapter by briefly diverting into the commencement of an *issues-driven* crisis, I recognize that what I have suggested looks distressingly like a checklist. That's because it is. Albeit a very short one. Sadly, I probably won't be popular for proposing such a thing. As surgeon Dr Atul Gawande notes in his superb book, *The Checklist Manifesto*, ambitious and clever people don't just mildly dislike checklists, their disregard for them is *visceral*.

He notes with exquisite accuracy why this is the case, reflecting that the use of them 'runs counter to deeply held beliefs about how the truly great among us – those who we aspire to be – handle situations of high stakes and complexity. The truly great are daring. They improvise. They do not have protocols and checklists' (Gawande 2009, p. 173).[6] I couldn't agree more with his observation. Nor could I agree more with his elegantly restrained observation that our view of heroism therefore needs reappraisal.

In the cognitive chaos of crisis, checklists reduce mental burden. That's why, as Captain Steven Hawkin's explains in his contribution to this chapter that pilots use them for *precisely* the purpose I counsel they are used for by organizational leaders; they slow the pace, assist with problem diagnosis, prevent premature intervention that may exacerbate the problem at hand and reassure followers of the crisis leader's grip of the situation, thus ensuring their effective and full contribution.

Using time and space when managing an issues-driven crisis

Before I conclude this chapter and outline the skills needed move *beyond* the commencement of crisis leadership, I need to take a brief diversion into that most vexing of crisis – the 'issues-driven crisis'.

Issues-driven crises are those for which there is no obvious starting point. There is no crash or bang. They develop slowly, sometimes imperceptibly and typically (if not exclusively) find their origins in either emerging *performance* failures or (possible) changes in *policy* implemented because of a shift in societal expectations.

The former is *typically* (but not exclusively) associated with *internal* failures. This can be anything from governance failures such as *systemic fraud* and *corruption* through to the more ephemeral challenges of, say, *poor morale*. The latter is *typically* (but again not exclusively) associated with changes in an organization's *external* environment, be it legislative change or a change in stakeholders' expectation of what an organization does and how it does it. This can be in relation to anything from the organization's approach to the 'gig economy' to executive pay to aggressive tax planning to the use of outsourced or overseas manufacturing.

What *unites* issues-driven crises and incident-driven crises is their ability to threaten the viability of the organization or present serious obstacles in the pathway to achieving its strategic objectives. Or, in other words, to precipitate a crisis. Fraud and corruption, for example, can lead to huge fines and exclusion from future opportunities. Protests against an organization's tax planning can lead to product or service boycotts or the materially increased costs that accompany greater regulatory or political scrutiny.

What *divides* them is the difference in the presence and use of time and space. In incident-driven crises, time and space are in short supply. Issues become crises because the leadership has, typically, had *too much* time and space.

The absence of a burning platform to act, combined with a series of personal and organizational blinkers, often leads to a failure to commence activities to mitigate the potential impact of the issue early enough. Thus the organization finds itself ultimately having to exercise crisis leadership because it finds itself in a corner with a slowly diminishing set of strategic options (as outlined

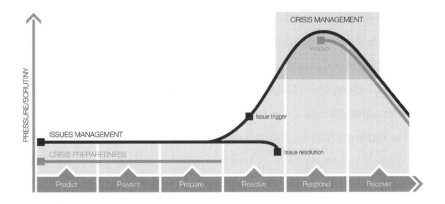

FIGURE 3.2 *The lifecycle of an issue-driven crisis. Adapted from Griffin, A. (2014),* **Crisis, Issues and Reputation Management.** *London: Kogan Page.*

in Figure 3.2) as the noise of the amplification factors grows. In short, the leadership has failed to prevent a crisis.

This happens for very many reasons. While it's unusual for an organization to entirely overlook an issue (which may have the potential to become a crisis), it's frequently the case that they fail to grip the situation early enough. This can be because of:

- **an unwillingness to tolerate open discussion of 'risk issues'.** The banking crisis of 2008 did not appear entirely without warning. Many eminent economists and investors, including economist Paul Krugman and market investor and hedge fund manager Michael Burry, who was so powerfully portrayed by Christian Bale in *The Big Short*, Hollywood's adaptation of Michael Lewis 2010 book of the same name, correctly identified the US banking sectors' exposure to sub-prime mortgages.[7]

- **the barriers to change are viewed as undesirable (or insurmountable).** The strength of the human commitment to maintaining the status quo is breathtaking. Organizations and their leadership typically abhor change. That's understandable. Change is exhausting. But, it can be utterly necessary. The notion, for example, that the rise of downloadable music could be stopped now seems laughable. Yet, that is precisely what the music industry attempted to do in the early 2000s. Until very recently, key oil-exporting countries denied that the *fracking* technology developed in the United States to extract shale oil from rocks would fundamentally change the global oil market. But, it did. As their incomes plunged, some tried to flood the market to drive these latter-day American pioneers (which initially had much higher costs) to the wall by forcing the price of oil down even further. It is now, of course, widely accepted that this strategy didn't work. Many of those countries have now accepted this view and are moving to diversify their economies away from their dependence on the exportation of hydrocarbons. Change prompted by the market fundamentals of supply and demand is like water, it will find a way through.

- **or there is, quite simple, nearly always something more pressing to do.** The outcome of this is no different. However, the cause is simply that in busy organizational lives, something else was, well, just more urgent.

Because there is no single reason as to why organizational leaders allow themselves to drift listlessly from dealing with what began as benign issue to battling the amplification factors of a crisis, there is no single answer to avoiding it. However, that doesn't mean organizational leadership is helpless. There are steps that can be taken.

Organizational emotional intelligence

Clearly organizations need to ensure that they are in the best possible position to spot the kernel of an issue at the earliest possible stage.

From an *internal* perspective, so much of this depends on the sorts of 'just culture' and 'high-reliability' behaviours I have urged leaders to promote within their organizations in Chapter 2. The simple act of encouraging (and indeed appropriately celebrating) the sharing of bad news ensures that issues which have the potential to develop into crises will be spotted so much earlier in the life cycle.

The constant assessment of the *external* environment is though critical, particularly to avoid the development of *policy-related* issues.

It is becoming increasingly common for political commentators to describe the environment organizations are now operating in as VUCA (which is short for *volatile, uncertain, complex* and *ambiguous*), a phrase which finds its roots in military parlance.[8] The United Kingdom's 2016 referendum to exit the European Union, followed by the election of Donald Trump to the US presidency are, as well documented, reflections of the shifts in societal expectations and ones which may have a profound impact on organizational performance.

This doesn't just require a passive interest in politics and a close eye on newspaper leaders and the 'commentariat'. It requires emotional intelligence at an *organizational level*. And this means engaging in conversation and dialogue with investors, community groups, competitors, lobby groups and the other critical stakeholders whose support is required (or whose opposition should be avoided). The earlier organizations understand what, if any, changes in expectation of what they do or how they do it, the earlier they can decide for themselves what, if anything, they want to do in response.

Creating a burning platform

However, identifying an issue and correctly assessing it as an existential threat to the organization is only the first step. The next is to galvanize the organization into action. And, this requires the creation of a 'trigger point' or a 'burning platform'. A metaphorical 'bang', perhaps. In a curious quirk it requires us to compel the organization to think that time and space is *not* on its side. It requires the simulation of a 'lite' version of the amplification factors or a 'trigger point' in the issues life cycle. Urgency is needed.

The way to do that depends utterly and entirely on the organization and the key decision makers and what, if any, scepticism exists as to the severity of the threat.

The sorts of tactics that can be employed are typically either hard and *quantitative* such as the use of externally commissioned surveys, reports, analysis into attitudes and views of the organization among its stakeholders. Gap analyses of how the organization performs in contrast to its peers in relation to the threat are a very popular platform. There is something oddly scary for many leaders about being different to their competitors, despite the need for competitive differentiation. Or they may be softer in nature. The use of a respected external, third-party expert or the formation of a coalition of people within the organization to compel other senior decision makers into action may be also be deployed.

All too often though, the necessary 'trigger point' required to galvanize the organization into action – and into appointing a crisis leader in line with the crisis management plans or something similar – comes from *external* sources. And, the list of what they can be is endless, ranging from a media expose – a regulatory sanction, a political intervention, labour unrest or a customer backlash. Or a combination of any of the above.

Whether the trigger was initiated internally or occurs from the external world, this brief but necessary diversion is over. The space and time that is so necessary for effective crisis leadership may remain in greater supply in an issues-driven crisis than it is in its incident-driven cousin. However, this trigger point is the moment at which the skills required of the crisis leader are the same, irrespective of whether the crisis has its origins in an incident or an issue. No further diversions are required, and the checklist I bravely offered earlier in this chapter can be consulted in (almost) exactly the same way as it can in an incident-driven crisis.

Conclusion

I have covered a lot of ground in this chapter. I have outlined how leaders overcome the challenges faced in the potentially overwhelming opening hours of an incident-driven crisis and exposed the very different challenges faced by those leaders who want to galvanize an early response to an issues-driven crisis. The overarching purpose of the chapter has been to ensure that the crisis leader has secured the *time* and *space* to tackle the challenges that will come in the hours, days and weeks ahead. In Chapter 4 I tackle one of the most difficult that of: decision-making and setting strategic direction.

COMMENCING CRISIS LEADERSHIP

Lessons from the cockpit: An interview with Captain Steve Hawkins

Whenever I discuss the notion of effective crisis leadership, commercial airlines pilots are quickly cited as being obvious role models for all those leaders who may one day have to lead in a crisis. There are countless reasons for that. Hollywood probably plays a role. But, so too does the brutal recognition that we rely, utterly, on airline pilots to address problems, small and large, with ruthless efficiency whenever we fly. Our lives depend on it.

And, of course, they surpass our expectations. Like a jet aircraft, the aviation safety statistics defy gravity. So, what lies at the root of this success and what can organizational leaders learn from it? I sat down with Captain Steve Hawkins, Chief Training Pilot at British Airways (BA), to find out.

Captain Hawkins is the very essence of a British Airways pilot. He is a tall, elegantly dressed man. And, he greets me with a firm handshake, saying 'good afternoon' in that voice pilots seem to be gifted with and which they use to so reassuringly welcome you aboard their aircraft. And, it is in that calming tone that he goes on to give invaluable advice to crisis leaders which is as relevant in the boardroom as it is in the cockpit.

He begins by explaining that central to pilot training are what is known as 'human factors'. These are the *non-technical* skills a pilot requires. And, within 'human factors' are two critical concepts: 'Threat and Error Management' (TEM) and 'Crew Resource Management' (CRM). The names don't matter, but what sits behind them does.

He explains that despite the huge resilience and *redundancies* built into modern aircraft, systems errors and mistakes are viewed as inevitable. That is the basis of TEM, which is concerned less with threat elimination and more

with the management of 'threats'. Pilots are taught to assume that they will, at
some point, have to demonstrate crisis leadership.

CRM relates to the leadership style pilots deploy, explains Captain Hawkins.
It emerged in the 1970s when the introduction of cockpit voice recorders
proved that aircraft accidents were caused not by poor flying ability, but often
because captains were reacting inappropriately to emerging problems. They
failed to harness the skills of the co-pilot and wider crew to diagnose the
problem and to manage it.

Today the image of the hero pilot dishing out orders is not only frowned
upon, it isn't allowed. Pilots are rigorously trained to marshal the capabilities of
the whole crew, cabin attendants included, when responding to unanticipated
problems.

It is hard to overstate the importance that Captain Hawkins places on the
diagnosis phase of 'commencing crisis leadership', that does not mean that
decisiveness is not important. On the contrary. Pilots who become *captains*,
he says, are those who, when faced with a potential crisis, can build on their
diagnostic skills to create *viable solutions* and ultimately decide on a course of
action.

However, to gain command (and maintain it) they have to prove to Captain
Hawkins that they can do this while demonstrating some of the behaviours
associated with CRM and while battling against the sort of amplification
factors a crisis brings (and, of course, also while deploying their technical flying
skills). The sorts of behaviours he cites ranges from 'considers suggestions from
others', 'recognises signs of stress, fatigue and overload in self and in others'
and 'delegates tasks appropriately and effectively'.

Recognizing that these behaviours are patently as relevant to the boardroom
as to the cockpit, I press Captain Hawkins to outline what advice he would give
to any crisis leader about to commence crisis leadership. He reply is as crisp
and neat as a BA uniform:

1. Learn to interpret a range of information sources. Constantly.

To adapt an old (aviator's) saying, a superior leader uses superior judgement to avoid situations that require the use of superior skill. Constantly scan information from a range of sources. Be alive to minor changes that could lead to major consequences. Spot and mitigate a crisis at its earliest stages.

2. Find time to assess options.

Find or create time to allow a full diagnosis of an emerging problem. Acting too quickly means potentially diagnosing the wrong problem and reducing options available. Captain Hawkins counsels: 'If leaders do things half as fast as they think they should, they'll still be doing them twice as fast as they need to'.

3. Don't centralize power.

Throughout the entire process, use the entire team. Enshrine a 'Just Culture', encourage everyone to raise matters of concern and seek the views of everyone, whatever the pressure, before making key decisions. This requires huge emotional intelligence and constant practice.

4. Minimize confirmation bias.

Confirmation bias (i.e. seeking information which confirms our instinct rather than counters it) is hardwired into us. It simply has to be managed. Leaders must ask open not closed questions, and avoid leading questions altogether. The aim is to enable others to develop and share an independent perspective rather than subconsciously encouraging them to reinforce your own.

5. Delegate to create strategic capacity.

Leaders need to delegate operational tasks (for a captain this can include handing flying the plane to the co-pilot) to free them to complete problem diagnosis and to use the time they have created to consider their options.

6. Use checklists to reduce the cognitive load.

Stress and adrenaline interfere with memory and cause oversights. Use checklists to ensure crucial tasks are not overlooked but also so that mental capacity can be expended elsewhere.

7. But be flexible and creative.

Checklists are vital but won't provide the whole answer. Exploit the mental capacity they have unlocked to think strategically and ahead. Even if the situation appears to have been remedied, scenario-plan every step of the response, until the crisis is unequivocally resolved. For a pilot this means the plane is at an airport gate and passengers have disembarked.

8. Be 100 per cent clear who is doing what.

There should be no doubt what task is being done and by whom. Ask those to whom tasks have been allocated to acknowledge their task and confirm it's been done.

9. Manage your body language

Teams look for every sign of reassurance from their leader in challenging circumstances. Leaders should maintain eye contact and not raise their voice, unless they have consciously chosen to do so.

10. Know yourself and your own stress triggers.

Know yourself and the signals that indicate you are working at capacity, and seek ways to reduce the mental burden. Where feasible, take a break. The crisis leader must, wherever possible, be operating at peak performance from the onset to the conclusion of a crisis.

For purists, there is a difference between 'emergency response' activities and the 'crisis management'. The work of flight crew is the former not the latter. But, at times, such differentiation doesn't matter. This is one of those times.

What is worth reflecting on is the sheer difficultly of executing Captain Hawkins advice. That's why all BA flight crew have to prove they can demonstrate exemplary crisis leadership skills every six months to the satisfaction of his exacting standards. If they can't, they can't fly.

That's why the safety statistics defy gravity. That's why we put our faith in Captain Hawkins and his colleagues so readily. And, that's why airline pilots are the role model of choice for so many potential crisis leaders.

4

The challenges of making decisions and setting (early) strategy

You are at a dinner party anywhere in the world. The food is good and the company excellent. New friends have been made, common acquaintances found and everyone has updated each other on the quotidian basics of life. Now the moment has arrived for those present to drift onto the news items of the day.

This is done cautiously at first; reactions need to be gauged. Sooner or later, however, a company, political party, charity or celebrity in crisis (by which I mean attracting negative media and social media comment) will enter conversation. Inevitably, someone will say the words: 'What they need to do is …'.

In doing this, one of the most powerful bodies in human society – the *court of public opinion* – is, in effect, casting its verdict on the response to the crisis by whatever or whoever is perceived to have caused it (or is responsible for the response to it).

To this powerful body – to which we are all periodically members – the answers are obvious. The leaking oil well simply needs to be blocked; the terrorists just need to be stopped; and the banks just need to go back to doing what they did in 'the good old days'.

The problem with the solutions presented is not that they are wrong. At least not necessarily. The problem is that they are, typically, too simplistic. They are influenced by a media required to give a black-and-white view of the world – and restricted to giving a tiny percentage of relevant information about a situation. The result is that the court of public opinion believes that simple, transactional solutions exist for grotesquely difficult challenges.

The world is not, as the popular media would have us believe, straightforward. The reality is that if there was an easy and straightforward answer to the 'crisis' under question, then the leader or leaders involved would have found it and fixed it. But if there was an easy answer then it wouldn't be a crisis. Any 'solution' in a crisis is likely to be partial, is likely to be imperfect and it will involve trade-offs. Sadly, the critical questions crisis leaders face when approaching decisions and setting the strategic path going forward is which trade-offs are the least bad. At very least in the short term.

However, that is not to say that crisis leaders should throw their hands in the air and descend into a spiral of handwringing defeatism. There is plenty a leader can and should think about when it comes to this most challenging area of leadership. And that is what this chapter sets out to explore.

I do this in two parts:

- **Part one** sets the context for decision-making in a crisis at both an organizational and personal level. At this personal level, I urge crisis leaders to have confidence, to exhibit four high-performing crisis leadership behaviours and to be resilient and disciplined in their approach. To help crisis leaders with this,

- **Part two** introduces a three-step model for crisis decision-making, the key tenets of which are 'sense, mission, containment' and helps lead to an (early-stage) strategic approach.

The model I outline in part two touches on the longer-term future too, in a nod to the fact that organizational leaders must make decisions about the strategy that they set for the long term. However, I address that in detail in Chapter 8. The focus of this chapter is to help guide leaders through the opening hours and days of a crisis, before they can give significant consideration to the future.

PART ONE

The effective use of time and space

In Chapter 3, I counselled that leaders need time and space in the opening moments of crisis leadership and I gave guidance on how to achieve it. Having achieved it, it is the responsibility of the leader to retain it and use it effectively. And, a critical part of that is making decisions and setting early-stage strategy, in both incident-driven and issues-driven crises.

However, just because leaders have secured time and space does not mean that the amplification factors, or indeed a variation on them, won't continue. They will, whether the crisis leader is about to chair a meeting of the CMT in an incident-driven crisis or is about to embark on a longer mission of tackling an issues-driven crisis. The amplification factors which, in my experience, most affect decision-making and strategy, will originate from four places:

- **The external environment**: When advising my clients in the early stages of a crisis, I warn them that, like a drama in the finest Shakespearean tradition, a series of characters will make their way onto the stage in the days and weeks ahead. There will be victims, villains, heroes and anti-heroes, traitors, jesters and narrators. The audience will be more akin to those the Bard would have known in the sixteenth century than the reserved type we know in 'business-as-usual' circumstances. They will laugh, clap, applaud, boo, hiss and cry. There will be a cacophony of noise, some of which should be listened to, but much of which should be ignored.

- **The organization:** An emerging crisis will prompt a range of internal responses in the affected organization. In my experience, organizations rally to the response, particularly in safety- and security-related crises. The antecedents to these are typically perceived to have lain outside the control of the organization (even if some level of culpability is ultimately established), and if the steps recommended in Chapter 2 have been followed. However, the appearance of old foes of the appointed crisis leader(s), using the situation for their own advancement, must be expected.

- **The problem:** In his book *Team of Teams*, General Stanley McChrystal differentiates complicated problems (problems that have many parts, with the parts joined in relatively simple, predictable ways) from problems that are complex (problems that have highly interactive parts. The interactions between the parts are nonlinear; they are unpredictable and defy our intuition.)[1] Crises are not always the latter, but they often are. I return to this later in the chapter in more detail.

- **The crisis leaders own personal demons:** Of course, there will always be the crisis leaders' own personal demons, or 'overdone strengths' as they are so often tactfully referred to. We are, of course, the Daniel Goleman generation of emotionally controlled leaders. And, while we may have successfully countered the amygdala's hijack when first informed about the crisis, the amplification factors still exert huge pressure. This leaves us exposed to working 'in the grip of the daimon', as psychologist Carl Jung wrote (Jung 1989, p. 356).[2] That makes us more prone to an endless list of 'defence mechanisms', as shown in Figure 4.1 below, and more likely to lean on heuristics (or rules of thumb) that we use to get through daily life. And, indeed they typically suffice in daily life, but not so in a crisis.

1. Denial – 'the expressed refusal to acknowledge a threatening reality of realities'

2. Disavowal – 'acknowledging a threatening reality but downplaying its importance'

3. Fixation – 'the rigid commitment to a particular course of action or attitude in dealing with a threatening situation'

4. Grandiosity – 'the feeling of omnipotence'

5. Idealization – 'ascribing omnipotence to another person, object, organization'

6. Intellectualization – 'the elaborate rationalization of an action or thought'

7. Projection – 'attributing unacceptable actions or thoughts to others'

8. Splitting – 'the extreme isolation of different elements, extreme dichotomization, or fragmentation'.

FIGURE 4.1 *Typical defence mechanisms observable in a crisis.*
Source: Mitroff and Pauchant, 1992, p.74.[3]

These four factors lead crisis leaders to be exposed to what some academics refer to as 'choking under pressure'.[4]

What crisis leaders must do to avoid this choking is to use the time and space they have created to step up and out of the crisis and look across the totality of it. They need to make decisions and set direction from outside the crisis rather than choke on it from the inside. Expressed in that term which is in danger of being overused (but which is very important in a crisis), decision-making and strategy setting mean leaders need to 'take a step back'.

And, no it's not easy. Far from it. It requires, in my experience, three things:

1. **Confidence**: Crisis leaders need to take confidence in their abilities as decision makers and strategy setters. It's what they do every day; it's different but the same.

2. **Behaviours**. They need to lean on four high-performance leadership behaviours; they need to be themselves but with more skill.[5]

3. **Resilience and Discipline**. They need to pursue a logical and comprehensive approach to the task. Their resilient use of discipline should underpin (but not curtail) their approach.

They are presented sequentially as each gives crisis leaders greater ability to deliver the next. I therefore examine each in turn.

1 Confidence: It's different but the same

One of the central arguments of this book is that leadership tasks required in a crisis are not different to the leadership tasks at any other time. Rather, the barriers to doing them well are so much harder and the consequences of getting them 'wrong' can be so far reaching. Nowhere is this drawn into sharper focus than when tackling decision-making and setting strategic direction.

These two competencies are, of course, inextricably and symbiotically linked. It's impossible to know which comes first. However, let's dissect them both and give them both due consideration. In doing so, I hope to show that decision-making and setting strategic direction in a crisis isn't vastly different from 'business as usual'.

Confidence in being 'the decider'

Although 'decision-making' is a term we use daily, *Harvard Business Review* editors, Leigh Buchanan and Andrew O' Connell, point out that it was a term restricted to public administration until the early twentieth century. It then entered the corporate world where it replaced terms such as 'resource allocation' and 'policy making'. Buchanan and O'Connell beautifully describe contemporary decision-making as a 'palimpsest of intellectual disciplines: mathematics, sociology, psychology, economics, and political science' (Buchanan and O'Connell 2006).[6]

Moreover, it involves emotion. The prominent US neuroscientist Antonio Damasio has shown the fundamental role emotions play in human functioning, particularly in our ability to make decisions in any circumstances let alone a crisis.[7]

So, decision-making is an activity that deserves our respect, but perspective has to be maintained. Leaders at every level in every organization make decisions. It is what they do, all day every day. The more senior leaders become, the more complicated and wide ranging the problems they have to solve are. Putting ourselves in positions in which the problems we have to solve and the decisions we have to make become ever greater – rather than ever easier – is a curious quirk of the human condition.

If you ask leaders above a certain level of seniority what motivates them, it's rarely financial remuneration. The most senior of leaders have long stopped having to worry about meeting Maslow's most basic needs a long time ago.[8] Rather they will say it is 'the challenge' that motivates them, by which they mean they are entrusted to grapple with an evermore fiendish set of problems. This, in a nutshell, is professional progress.

The former US president Barack Obama addresses this topic beautifully in an interview with writer Michael Lewis. In it, Michael Lewis asks President Obama about the decisions he makes, and he references George W. Bush's description of the president as a *decider*. President Obama explains that nothing brought to his desk was perfectly solvable. If it was, someone else would have solved it. Instead, he dealt with probability – he acknowledges that any given decision he maed had a 30–40 per cent chance of failure.[9] This did not, I am sure, relieve him entirely of the burden of the agonizing choices he had to make during his presidency. But, it means he was working within the constraints of American political scientist Herbert Simon's notion of 'bounded rationality'; he accepted that *satisfactory*, rather than *optimal* was about the best he could achieve and was thus able to direct his energies accordingly. I return to this later.

We are, of course, not in the shoes of the president of the United States; the peace of the world does not rest on our shoulders. It clearly takes a special type of resilience to withstand that sort of pressure, and the example is only used for the purpose of explanation.

Such pressure is, however, also relative. It is experienced through the eyes of whoever the 'decider' is, and in relation to the support and resources available to him or her.

The problems presented to President Obama are geostrategic in nature, but 'POTUS' has the State Department, CIA and US military to respond to it. While the seemingly intractable problems brought to most leaders are not, the resources they have to fix them are also consummately smaller. Thus they may feel to us as the geostrategic conundrums did to President Obama when they landed on his desk. It's about relativity and context.

So whatever leaders are leading, deciding is what they do. All day, every day. And leaders should take confidence from that. The requirement on them has merely ratcheted up several notches.

Strategy is about uncertainty whatever the circumstances

If the media is over inclined to the use of the word crisis, then everyone involved in organizational life is certainly over inclined to the use of the word 'strategy'.

However, the point I wish to make is that the process of setting strategy in a crisis is not radically different to setting strategy in 'business as usual'.

Leaders trying to set strategy during a crisis, in my experience, are typically of the view that what makes it so hard is the sheer uncertainty of it all. However, there is no certainty in setting strategy in any circumstance.

As the famous Henry Mintzberg wrote, 'organizations have strategies to reduce uncertainty, to block out the unexpected, and … to set direction, focus effort and define the organization' (Mintzberg 1987, p. 29).[10] He wasn't writing about strategy setting in a crisis. And yet, he may as well have been.

What makes setting strategy so difficult in a crisis isn't the absence of certainty but rather the situational challenges brought about by two tightly bound amplification factors; the constantly and noisily presented *counterfactual* and the presence of *cognitive* dissonance. Let's deal with both.

In periods of 'business as usual', organizational leaders are kept on their toes through a cocktail of means. Communities upon whom the organization has an impact be they employees, customers or shareholders do, of course, voice their opinions on its activities. But it's typically done, in relative terms, gently. And frankly, if things are going well, few people trouble themselves with proffering a *counterfactual*, a term coined by the American philosopher Nelson Goodman in 1947.[11] In simple terms, counterfactual thinking is when we question outcomes by asking 'what might have happened if ...' or 'if only I had ...'.

Think of some of the world's most successful companies. Or football teams. Or indeed any institution and individual renowned for their success. Or even the best meal you have ever eaten.

Ask yourself if it's totally out of the question that they could be on could have been even better? Unlikely perhaps. But, it's not impossible. However, few people would be bothered spending time considering it.

However, in a crisis, suddenly, everyone has a noisy, public, passionate, (typically) ill-informed and often bad-tempered opinion on what is neatly described as the 'coulda, shoulda, woulda' (Zaremba 2009, p. 35).[12] Leaders aren't used to it.

And this leads to a screaming case of Leon Festinger's famous 1957 condition, *cognitive dissonance*, which is the stress and discomfort leaders feel when they are presented with conflicting information.[13]

The crisis itself creates the first wave of this. This product is safe. Surely? Then the twisting turning nature of a crisis has the potential to deliver further waves of it. Every time a decision is made, new information appears – or a counterfactual is presented by a noisy stakeholder. And, the leader falls potentially victim to an inner need to quieten the dissonance and restore psychological order.

This can lead to ineffective behaviours ranging from *cognitive inertia* (a reliance on familiar assumptions even if the evidence for them is no longer there) and the use of heuristics (rules of thumb) through to the infamous concept of *confirmation bias*, which is to search for information that justifies our views or serves to confirm what we already know, rather than search for and assess new information which may be genuinely useful.

So, setting strategy in a crisis – like making decisions – is a challenge. Everything is harder and tougher. It's all just 'more' (which is why it requires heightened discipline). However, the central message I give to leaders is that the substance of what they are being asked to do is no different; merely the circumstances in which they are doing it are more challenging. It's different but the same.

They should take confidence from that. Critically, they should simply seek to recognize the amplification factors for what they are. As ever, awareness is the first critical step in meeting any problem or challenge.

If they successfully do that, they are more likely to be able to deliver the four high-performance leadership behaviours I believe are pivotal to effective decision-making and to which I turn next.

2 Behaviours: Being yourself but with more skill

I said at the beginning of this book I would not present lists of attributes that make some crisis leaders more effective than others, and for the most part I have avoided that. However, in my experience, crisis leaders who are effective at making decisions and setting strategy execute four highly effective behaviours. Effective crisis leaders are:

- **Cognizant of, but not captured by, history and precedent:** one of the things that is most striking about the leaders I have seen make decisions and set strategy successfully is that they have a deep interest in previous – sometimes historical – crises that are similar or related.

  Talk to any of the key leaders involved in pandemic response either at pharmaceutical companies or multilateral public health institutions and you will find keen students of the 1918 flu pandemic, the deadliest in modern history, which killed an estimated 50 million people. It is constantly referenced.

  It's a point that the former Governor of the Bank of England, Lord (Mervyn) King, makes in his contribution to this chapter, and one that his fellow leaders in battling the 2008 banking crisis – Ben Bernanke, Hank Paulson and Timothy Geithner – all stress in their memoirs on the topic. Their understanding of the 1931 American Depression was pivotal in helping the world avoid the economic abyss of previous banking crises.

  What I have observed and noticed in my discussions with crisis leaders who have this intellectual curiosity is the great sense of balance with which they harness it. Of course they notice the similarities between the crisis they are involved in now and those they have studied (or been involved in previously). And, of course, this is helpful as it leads to great economies of decision-making. However, they avoid seeking similarities which aren't there. Rather, they notice what is different and thus avoid deploying the 'right measures' at the 'wrong time'. This is, of course, just as important. But it is much harder, as the cognitive effort in spotting the differences is greater than inelegantly retrofitting similarities of analysis and remediation. This brings me to my next observation, which is that effective crisis leaders must be:

- **Prepared to admit that they were wrong**: I have long been of the view that the greatest act of self-confidence in any leader – at whatever level and in whatever situation – is to concede that he or she has made a mistake. In a crisis this is an essential skill. No leader can make the right decision (insofar as one exists) every time.

  There are a huge number of decisions to be made in a crisis, all subject to changing information. As a result, the temptation to declare constant changes of direction is huge. That, of course, is not effective. Concessions of being wrong is a valuable commodity to be deployed with care. However, the economist John Maynard Keynes apparently once said, when he was accused of changing his position on a particular topic, 'When I find new information, I change my mind. What do you do?' (Earley 1979, p. 540).[14] This is a never-bettered, beautifully put justification. This humility is critical in and of itself, not least for the maintenance of leadership credibility with the wider CMT to whom it is often clear that something has or is 'going wrong'. It is, however, also indicative of the crisis leader's ability to be:

- **Open to creativity and challenging the status quo:** few people like change. And, fewer still like it during times of crisis. In my experience, most leaders attempt a flight to the status quo (to lower the cognitive dissonance). And, they do this at every stage of a crisis. But, crisis leaders must try and resist this. Those leaders who reveal an openness to creativity do not, for example, accept limits on what can be done to support victims and families during, say, a safety or security crisis even if the emergency services are providing primary care. And it's a willingness during performance- or policy-related crises to concede that, in the former, the organizational structures or strategies may be failing – or be in decline – and in the latter that, perhaps, other stakeholders have a valid point. Leaders don't want to do this because it's hard (and it opens to them even more cognitive dissonance). They display the cognitive equivalent of putting their hands over the ears, stamping their feet and declaring 'I'm not listening'. Such an approach is, of course, far from effective.

And, finally, crisis leaders need:

Resilience & discipline: days and weeks – and sometimes months – of counterfactuals and cognitive dissonance are, at the risk of understatement, exhausting. Leaders fall victim to what is known as *decision fatigue*. The term 'decision fatigue' was coined by American social psychologist Roy Baumeister, who explains how decision-making wears us down, consuming our limited mental stamina.[15] After making a series of choices our decision-making resource is depleted, leading to mental exhaustion. This fatigue can lead to less effective choices being made, or cases of decision avoidance. This exhaustion gives rise again to crisis leaders being in the arms of 'the grip' and at the mercy of a bias, with the temptation to hunt for the path of least (but often ineffective) resistance.

How leaders cope with this is a very personal matter. There is no single, magic bullet. However, resilience is a topic I return to in more detail in Chapter 7, when I explore the private, rather than public, aspects of crisis leadership.

No leader should try and be like any other leader. Every leader has to do things their own way. And some leaders will find the behaviours listed above easier to display than others. Certainly, no one will display them all with the same level of accomplishment all of the time. However, by identifying them and by encouraging leaders to continue to heed Goleman's counsel of being aware of their own behaviours – even under the most testing of circumstances – will, I hope, encourage leaders not to copy others or blindly follow lists of leadership attributes, but instead to adapt and blend them into their own behaviours. In short, to respond to Collin and Porras' now famous call to be themselves. But, with more skill.[16]

PART TWO: A DECISION-MAKING MODEL FOR CRISIS LEADERS

Decision-making and strategy setting

The second half of this chapter outlines a decision-making model which I believe provides the basis for making decisions and ultimately setting early-stage strategy. It is a model that can be used by a leader chairing meetings of the crisis management team during a rapidly moving, incident-driven crisis during which the initial stages of the process are concertinaed into a few days and weeks. Or it can be used by a leader overseeing the response over a period of a few weeks or months in small discursive groups tasked with fixing an issues-driven crisis.

Much of what is outlined ought to be staggeringly straightforward. The individual, sequentially addressed component parts are, of course, only really what senior leaders ought to be doing on a day-to-day basis as they plot the path for their organization. But that's the point and is, of course, one of the underlying premises of this book.

The challenge is that under the duress of a crisis, and because of the amplification factors outlined earlier, the discipline of execution deserts us (assuming it was there in the first place). Typically, individual parts of the process are short-circuited, they are undertaken in the wrong order or we fail to collaborate effectively both within each part or to smooth our path from one into the other.

(The point about collaboration is a critical one and is worthy of a brief side note. It is my strong belief that collaboration is fundamental to decision-making and strategy setting in a crisis. Although I touch on it in this chapter, I address it more fully in the next when I address team working. The separation of the two is unwelcome but necessary for clarity. This chapter and Chapter 5 should be read together closely; the latter brings to life the former).

The process is designed to ensure that through the possible brain fog courtesy of the amygdala, the amplification factors and, possibly, screaming cognitive dissonance, the crisis leader has a process to follow which is logical and which forces the maintenance of discipline during this most critical and, possibly, criticized requirement of crisis leadership. This is consistent with a core tenet of systems thinking which, in the face of complexity, encourages leaders to focus on the decision making process rather than the decision itself.

So what is involved?

A four-part process

I believe successful decision-making and strategy setting (see Figure 4.2) require leaders to (rapidly) collaborate in order to determine:

- **Sense:** this places the problem in terms of its impact on the organization and on others and, critically, in terms of the involvement of others in the response.

- **Mission:** this gives a purpose to the response.

- **Containment objectives**: this addresses the immediate crisis.

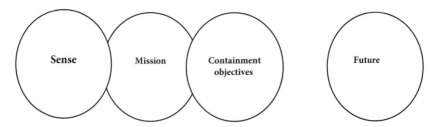

FIGURE 4.2 *The four-part decision-making and strategy-setting process.*

- **Future**: this assesses the long-term, post-crisis direction of the organization.

There is huge overlap with each. Crises don't fit neatly into boxes or silos, and nor do the processes to tackle them. However, clarity once again demands we investigate each in turn. I will now look at *sense, mission* and *containment* in depth, before concluding with a very brief word on the *future*. This will be covered in more detail in Chapter 8.

Sense

So many crises bring with them a sense of loss – whether that is a loss of life, a loss of money or a loss of status. It is only human nature to want to replace what has been lost, but there is much work to be done before the crisis leader can establish what exactly has been lost and how it can be replaced, if indeed it can be replaced at all.

Earlier in the chapter, I introduced McChrystal's notion of complex and complicated problems. However, crises can be even more challenging than that. Many theories have been developed over the years to try and categorize the most fiendishly challenging of problems, and explore how they might be tackled. The 1970s saw the extension of systems thinking, and in 1973 the term 'wicked problem' was coined by academics Horst Rittel and Melvin M. Webber.[17] It is closely linked to the term 'messes', a term attributed to American organizational theorist Russell L. Ackoff.[18]

Wicked problems were defined by John Camillus in an article for *Harvard Business Review* in 2008, in which he says that they are problems with

many stakeholders with different values; the roots of which are complex and tangled; the problem is difficult to come to grips with and changes at every attempt; there is no precedent and there is nothing to indicate the right answer to the problem. (Camillus 2008)[19]

Messes, on the other hand, are complex systems of problems which cannot be separated. Indeed, one of the underlying principles of systems thinking is that the problems they address shouldn't be deconstructed. Rather the totality of the problem should be examined.

On the face of it, this might appear to challenge the validity of the decision-making model I propose, which clearly does deconstruct the approach to crises into a segmented process. Possibly, but I would argue that not all crises are wicked problems or messes.

Keith Grint, a professor at the UK's Warwick University, differentiates *crisis problems* (which he believes do have a clear and finite solution) with *wicked problems* (which do not, and which critically involve multiple agencies).[20] There is merit in this separation.

However, what is important for the crisis leader is not whether they ascribe a theoretical and abstract category to a crisis but rather that they seek to:

- **understand the complexity of the crisis at hand and, accordingly, begin to rationalize what can be achieved.** A 1998 web article by academics Jeffrey Conklin and William Weil suggests that when it comes to wicked problems, leaders should build on the concept of bounded rationality I have introduced earlier, noting that the best leaders can hope for is satisficing.[21] Or, in other words, that satisfactory is better than optimal. Circumstances don't allow anything different. Similarly, Russell L. Ackoff counsels that when it comes to messes, a partial solution to the whole system of problems is better than a whole solution to each of its individual parts. This is because when leaders separate messes into their component parts, they lose their essential properties – meaning leaders are not actually tackling what they need to tackle.[22] And, related to that the crisis leader should:

- **identify which parties are involved, accept that they will have different views and that 'success' remains, to an extent, out of**

their hands. True crises typically involve dozens of impacted and responding organizations. They cannot be solved by one organization alone. This means that not only is the organization at the centre of it vulnerable to the competence of its fellow responders, it is at the mercy of the self-interest of those seeking to use the situation to promote their own aims. What is a crisis for one organization can be an opportunity for another. Cognitive scientist Douglas Hofstadter bravely proposed that the answer to this is 'superrationality', which he outlined in his 1986 book *Metamagical Themas*. When harnessing superrationality, everyone puts aside their own agenda in the response to a crisis.[23] However, finding an example of such a utopia in the real world is hard. *Realpolitik* is simply too powerful.

All of this sounds straightforward but really isn't – as former Governor of the Bank of England Lord King attests to in his contribution to this chapter. Rather than referring to wicked problems or messes, Lord King references a concept drawn from game theory – the *prisoner's dilemma*. He notes that during the 2008 financial crisis, many of the parties were subsumed under the prisoner's dilemma. The theory was popularized by Canadian mathematician Albert Tucker, and was originally put forward in 1950 by American mathematicians Merrill Flood and Melvin Dresher as part of the RAND Corporation's explorations into game theory. The basic idea of the prisoner's dilemma is that it's a sort of zero sum game in which, to avoid losing, both parties have to pursue a winning strategy even if the collective result is unproductive. King bemoans not having spotted this earlier.

The challenge is that leaders are typically wired to shoot for the stars and achieve an ideal outcome. The problem with so many crises – whether they qualify as wicked problems or not – is that so many of the variables lie outside their control. They cannot, for example, control the weather! Thus, leaders need to conserve their energy and work out where to focus their attention by correctly understanding the situation they face before launching into premature or overtly ambitious response initiatives which are destined to fail.

What crisis leaders need to do to achieve this depends, of course, on the nature of the crisis itself. However, in simple terms, they need firstly to understand how complex the crisis is and the universe of stakeholders involved in the response process. And to do that, crisis leaders need to be prepared to extend the basic diagnostic questions proposed in Chapter 3 (whose purpose in any case was largely to slow the pace rather than create *situational awareness*) to engage in something more akin to what American organizational theorist Karl E. Weick calls 'sense-making'.

Sense-making is the attempt to make sense of an ambiguous situation.

More precisely, sense-making is the process of creating situational awareness in situations of high complexity or uncertainty in order to make decisions. It is a 'motivated, continuous effort to understand connections (which can be among people, places, and events) in order to anticipate their trajectories and act effectively' (Klein, Moon and Hoffman 2006, p. 71).[24]

The practical steps involved in undertaking sense-making effectively and the output from it need not be highly complex. However, what is critical is that crisis leaders do not attempt sense making on their own. They need to work closely and effectively with members of the CMT in order that they do not miss critical considerations as they seek to determine situational awareness. For that reason I address how this should be done in detail in the following chapter when I explore high-performing crisis team leadership.

If leaders follow this advice and work with their CMT to understand *what has happened*, *who is involved* and the *interconnectedness which links those who are involved*, they will be in a good position to attempt the next step in the decision making process which is to determine their specific mission in the complex web of responding organizations.

Mission

In my experience, crisis leaders routinely battle with two biases when it comes to the role of their organization during a crisis. They either try to:

- overreach for control and undertake tasks for which they are simply not qualified; or

- abdicate responsibility, declaring the response to be the responsibility of others.

Let's call this 'intervention bias'. As with most things in life, rarely do leaders operate at the extremes of these biases. Typically, they lean towards one or the other. This is not to say that there is, necessarily, mal-intent here. A desire to overreach is often driven out of a profound desire to help, or to do *something*. Rarely have I met a crisis leader who doesn't want to fix a problem that his or her organization is perceived to have been instrumental in creating, irrespective of how involved it actually was.

However, a bias towards inaction, delayed intervention and/or abdication of responsibility sometimes does happen. The reasons for this range from a psychological response at the individual level of the leader, through to an overtly legalistic culture which pervades the organization and advocates a 'saying nothing, doing nothing and admitting nothing' approach (Regester and Larkin 2008, p. 199).[25] Typically, but not always, this results from the litigious scars borne by an organization from something that has gone before.

Other reasons often exist. Sometimes, through a failure of the sort of planning outlined in Chapter 2, a genuine confusion of roles exists among the universe of responders. This ambiguity leads to inertia or jostling for position.

Whatever the influencing factors, what is required of crisis leaders is that having mapped the universe of the response during the sense-making process, they move beyond these biases and seek to bring clarity from within the complexity by determining:

- **what the role of their organization is in the response effort,** and that they are therefore able to articulate, in very general terms:

- **what their mission is.**

The factors that affect this depend, of course, on the organization in crisis. The considerations for a company selling services to foreign governments are different to those driving, say, a charity. Moreover, the universe in which crisis leaders are responding is endlessly dynamic as the relationships between the parties wax and wane and as the court of public opinion assigns the role of victim and villain at times, seemingly, arbitrarily. *Sense-making* therefore requires constant reassessment.

However, intervention bias and a clear sense of mission should be determined by the crisis leader working his or her way through two moderating factors (as outlined in Figure 4.3), which are *expectation* and *limitation*.

I examine both in detail.

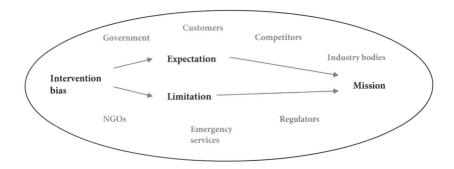

FIGURE 4.3 *Defining the response mission.*

Expectation

When it comes to expectation, crisis leaders need, in my experience, as early as possible, to understand two key points:

- **What is legally expected of us?** Surely, undertaking the very minimum of statutory requirements is straightforward? Who would want to do less? Very few leaders, in my experience; most want to do more. The challenge comes in working out precisely what is required. This is not always straightforward. Laws need interpreting; that's why lawyers exist. And, in many countries in the world, the body of law is far from robust. Nor is it overseen by a stable judiciary which works independently of its government. Plus, for international organizations, the issue of whose jurisdiction has *primacy* (as the authorities also battle for control) can be confounding in a crisis. In short, it is easy to fall foul of achieving even the minimum response, despite a desire to go beyond this. However, there is another even more complex factor to consider:

- **What do our stakeholders expect us to do?** Most crises occur because a gap has emerged between how an organization is expected to perform and how it has actually performed. An aeroplane is not expected to crash, a bank is not expected to fail nor a technology company to lose data. The affected organization must therefore work hard to minimize the gap between how its stakeholders expect it to respond and how it goes on to do so, therefore satisfying as many of the most important stakeholders as it can. Again, this is can be exceedingly challenging. I have heard many leaders fall back on the laudable vow to 'do the right thing'. But the right thing in whose eyes? Not all stakeholders will expect the same, so it won't be possible to satisfy them all. If there is one certainty that leaders can rely on, however, it is that the court of public opinion will expect more than the court of law.

Managing this balance is not easy, and it will create cognitive dissonance. But, it's not an optional task. It's the first critical step towards the generation of a mission. This must though be combined with the other moderating factor: limitation.

Limitation

To explore this factor, I am going to fall back once more on Griffin's typologies of different types of crises, as it is necessary to explore the different dynamics that emerge that are related to the notion of limitation. Such limitations take three forms – namely *ability*, *authority* and *appropriateness* – each of which is tightly woven into the types of crisis, which we will now explore.

Safety

In a safety crisis it is very often the responsibility of the responding emergency services to lead the response. That doesn't mean to say that there is no role for the affected organization. Lets use the example of a petro-chemicals company which has suffered a catastrophic fire at one of its plants. The plants owners or operators will be required to have their own response capability. So it's not entirely a case of ability as much as authority and indeed appropriateness which leads the emergency services to have 'primacy'. Our mission here is therefore to 'provide whatever support we can to the emergency services' – whatever those emergency services may be.

Security

The affected organization's role in a security crisis depends dramatically on what sort of security crisis is being faced. In a situation in which a terrorist atrocity has occurred – or is occurring – then clearly, or at least typically, it is only government resources which are able to respond and have the authority do so. And indeed, that is only appropriate. Our mission here then again becomes one of 'supporting the authorities'. In a breach of cyber security by terrorists or nefarious criminals, it is the directly affected organization which is typically able and most appropriately positioned to respond, even though there is an ever-growing thicket of legislation governing the which influences how this is done. The affected organisations mission here therefore is 'to contain the incident as quickly as possible, liaising closely with the authorities'.

Performance

A performance crisis is similar in dynamic to a cyber crisis, albeit (probably) much slower in its development, insofar as it is likely to be left to the crisis leader or whoever is appointed by the crisis leader to grip the crisis and to fix it. This is typically appropriate and the leader should be able to do so. However, authority can easily change. Institutional shareholders (represented by the board or chair) may, for example, exert their power and call for different crisis leadership if the affected organisation is a listed company. At the same time, regulators may invoke special measures. In extremis, administrators may take control. However, in the initial stages at least, the affected organization's mission is to 'respond to concerns and tackle the (emerging) crisis immediately at its root cause'.

Policy

It is in this typology that the limitations are most acute for the organisation(s) most affected. This is not due to the intangible nature of the crisis but, more critically, the numerous number of stakeholders involved. A policy crisis is, of all the typologies, most likely to be a *wicked problem* or a *mess* from the very beginning. The *ability* to fix the crisis lies in the hands of many, the *authority* to fix it is opaque, and the *appropriateness* of anyone's intervention depends on multiple and changing factors. What's more, the gift of declaring the crisis to be 'fixed' is in stakeholders' hands, not the affected organization's. In this typology, the affected organization's mission is either to defend its position effectively and thus successfully resist policy changes, or adapt effectively to a new policy environment. The organization is thus taking on the baton of persuasion or that of (potentially) far-reaching internal change. Neither is easy or appealing.

To be clear, I am not arguing that any CMT requires an elegantly crafted mission statement. Rather I am arguing that, given all of the points outlined above, organizations need a clear sense of their general mission in response to the crisis. The crisis leader needs to be able to complete, with conviction and clarity, the following sentence: 'In the response to the crisis that we face, our role is … '.

Unless the crisis leader can do that, he or she will be unable to tackle the next critical element of the process and that is to form containment objectives.

Containment objectives

Most crisis management teams – or at least those which practise and are prepared – conduct their meetings surrounded by white boards which display critical information. This is a good thing. The simple act of writing things down has innumerable benefits, about which I say more in Chapter 5.

What is included on those boards, however, depends entirely on the organization and the type of crisis the organization is likely to face. There will though invariably be a space for *objectives* – details on what the crisis management team is trying to achieve. However, I have lost count of the number of times I have entered the crisis management team room and, where objectives should be written, there is only a blank space.

But why? There is no leader of any part of any organization anywhere in the world who would not declare the importance of clearly stated objectives, whether that's for the whole organization, an individual department, a single project or indeed a particular employee. And yet when clarity is of paramount importance, they are missing. Why?

It can, of course, reflect the poor execution of the steps above, which leads to a lack of clarity from the leadership. However, in my experience, leaders often resist crafting objectives and there are multiple reasons why they do this. In my experience, it's typically because:

- **It's hard work.** The objectives that appear in any business-as-usual presentation or document in most organizations do not, at face value, do justice to the months of research and consultation that sit behind them. Identifying and agreeing on objectives is difficult. As Daniel Kahneman says, we are inherently lazy and use 'system one' thinking quickly and intuitively in preference to exerting the effort that 'system two' thinking requires.[26] And that's without the challenges of a crisis. In any crisis, the brain fog of the amygdala, combined with the amplification factors faced, heightens the risk that we avoid the cognitive dissonance that comes in trying to define our objectives and instead we succumb to the path of least resistance, engaging in action for the satisfaction of the (apparent) progress it brings but without any coherent insight into what we are trying to achieve.

- **It provokes conflict with others.** Not only does setting objectives create internal conflict within individual leaders, it creates conflict with fellow CMT members. Or at least it has the potential to do so. The ambiguous nature of a crisis means this risk is hardwired into the situation. Once again, our desire to create harmony wins.

- **It slows things down.** For so many crisis leaders, stopping and slowing down to undertake tasks such as objective setting (as well as sense-making) provokes an internal reaction that is akin to a painful one. But the strategic crisis leader's role – as opposed to the emergency response leader – is not to save life or protect the environment through sudden and immediate intervention. Just *doing* for the strategic leader is not heroic. It is evidence of the emotional hijack I have discussed in Chapter 3.

But, however difficult, each has to be battled. Not so rigidly as to set an unbending course. Crises don't work like that. Too much lies outside the control of the crisis leader. As Henry Mintzberg also wrote, 'setting oneself on a predetermined course in unknown waters is the perfect way to sail straight into an iceberg' (Mintzberg 1987, p. 26).[27] However, a stated set of objectives, however broad, built upon a pragmatic and realistic understanding of the mission of your organization, will supercharge the strategic response and lift the effectiveness of the crisis leader just when it is most required.

It will do this for many reasons. The process of setting objectives in and of itself will re-engage the higher cognitive functions of the leader and the team, provide reassurance among the team and confidence in the leader and provide the team with an *esprit de corps* and sense of purpose.

However, most importantly of all, containment objectives are critical pieces of what University of Chicago economist Richard H. Thaler, and Harvard Law School professor Cass R. Sunstein call 'choice architecture'.[28] What do I mean by that?

Containment objectives: Some frameworks and some options

To explore this, it's necessary to explore, briefly, some examples of 'containment' objectives. Most have relatively generic origins at their foundation, and these are shown in Figure 4.4.

Crisis is yet to happen	Crisis has happened and is in progress	Crisis has happened and is over.
Prevent it (either by blocking it or adapting)	Stop it.	Accept it.
Prepare to remediate impact.	Remediate impact.	Remediate impact.
Prevent recurrence (of similar threat).	Prevent immediate recurrence.	Prevent immediate recurrence.

FIGURE 4.4 *Containment objectives.*

Specificity comes with the nature of the crisis, its sector of origin and the organization's mission. However, for an oil company responding to a spill, they might be: *protect and support people who are affected, protect the environment, protect our rigs and equipment* and *protect our financial position and limit legal liability.*

And it's here that not only the value of the objectives but the order of priority in which they are addressed becomes so apparent.

If proposals are, for example, brought to provide support to the local communities impacted by the oil spill but which require significant investment, the objectives listed in priority order provide a clear guiding light on the decision to be taken. That doesn't mean that there shouldn't be discussion on how much should be invested and which of the proposals brought to the crisis leader should be accepted. (Not least because they should be challenged for appropriateness). However, had there been no objectives – or the objectives been listed in the opposite order – then the decision on the proposals may have been very different.

The complexity of a crisis means that the crisis leader will be constantly faced with decisions such as these. Having objectives which are as clear as possible and, wherever possible, listed in priority order, give the crisis leader one of the greatest tools he or she has to call upon, which is the ability to be able to say: 'I don't know the answer. But, based on what we know and what we are trying to achieve, I think we should… .'

Future

Much is made in crisis management circles about the Chinese word for 'crisis' (wēijī), which means both 'opportunity' and 'danger'. Crisis management professionals on the speaker circuit reveal the link to delegates with solemn aplomb, as if it was the greatest discovery since universal gravitation.

Quite apart from the fact that the correct use of the Chinese word is now widely refuted (and that crisis management speakers therefore need to change their slides), there are few opportunities in these opening days (and possibly weeks) of a crisis. They do exist; tales of great achievement from great adversity are not short in supply. Sometimes they come from actions taken during the 'containment phase'. Niche and extraordinary feats of engineering developed under the pressure of a crisis to put out the fire or recover trapped people, for example, may be displayed. However, typically, the potential to realize true *opportunity* exists once the containment phase is over and the organization has effectively contained the crisis. Containing it successfully is, in and of itself, the opportunity.

There are though, of course, no fluid lines here. Often the antecedents of opportunity can be found in the containment phase. And, there are a number of 'bridging activities' which link one to the other. Typically, these are the investigations and reviews that most organizations begin as quickly as they can, either of their own accord or under the direction of regulators or prosecutors, to uncover the root cause of the crisis. What is recommended in the conclusions of these swiftly produced reports can be placed along a spectrum which ranges from repairing the status quo (but with key incremental operational changes) through to profound change which is akin to a 'new future' for the organization at the centre of the crisis. Any one of the recommendations made along the specturm may be an opportunity. Or presented as such.

However, while it's tempting to look at the 'future', in whatever form it may take for the purpose of completeness, crises need to be contained first. For that reason, I will return to this in detail in Chapter 8, when I address the complexities of ending crisis leadership. The intervening chapters will address the challenges of crisis leadership that will continue until that point has been reached.

Conclusion

That most famous of strategists, Prussian soldier Carl Von Clausewitz, once said that everything in strategy is simple, but that doesn't mean that everything is easy. And in no situation is that truer than when making decisions and setting strategy in a crisis. Rarely though does Clausewitz appear at dinner parties to explain the conundrum faced by leaders to the court of public opinion.

I have set out what is essentially a straightforward process, and following that process is critical. I have simply counselled crisis leaders to know what's going on, understand their role in fixing it and know what they are trying to achieve. What is hard about that?

Nothing. At least not on paper. But the practical difficulties of executing it are enormous. Matthew Syed, in *Black Box Thinking*, believes that 'Intelligence and seniority when allied to cognitive dissonance and ego is one of the most formidable barriers to progress in the world today' (Syed 2015, p. 116).[29]

There are no silver bullets to offer crisis leaders. But what crisis leaders do have is the wider CMT or the colleagues they work with to respond to the crisis. The way crisis leaders collaborate with them is pivotal to bringing the process outlined above to life. And, in doing so, to making effective decisions and setting realistic strategies. For that reason, that's what I tackle in Chapter 5.

DECISION-MAKING IN A CRISIS

Lessons from the Old Lady of Threadneedle Street: An interview with Lord Mervyn King

The gently rolling green hills of the English county of Kent are a far cry from the agitated, paranoid, grey hustle and bustle of London's financial district. Yet, this is where Lord (Mervyn) King of Lothbury, the former governor of the Bank of England now spends much of his time. That is between jetting around the world to meet his academic obligations at various elite universities.

It was here, on a beautiful summer morning, that I met Lord King to discuss the issue of leadership decision-making in a crisis. As the governor of the Bank of England from 2003 to 2013, he led the institution during one of the most acute and complex crises it had ever endured, the 2008 global financial crisis. Who better to assess the challenges of crisis decision-making than him. So, over pots of English breakfast tea, what lessons would he share?

Meeting as we did in the former governor's beautifully curated library, it ought to be no surprise that one of the first points Lord King made is the importance he attaches to understanding the past to understand the present.

For Lord King, crisis leaders gain enormously from the diligent study of crises that have affected their organizations or industries in the past. This, he believes, frees the mind and allows the leader to be an *expert in imagination* and gives them crucial *intellectual self-confidence* both of which are in such high demand when there are so many different agendas and priorities that typically accompany a crisis. Indeed, he noted that throughout the crisis, he referred as much to the *history* of financial crises, as he did the mathematical models drawn up for him by his staff.

That is not to say that specific answers to contemporary crises are likely to be found purely in historical examples. On the contrary. The governor was at pains to stress that no two crises are the same and that there is no such thing as a *generic crisis*.

It was during this early part of our discussion that Lord King emphasized just how important it is, at the outset of any crisis, for the leader to establish just what is going on.

While this sounds simple on paper, crises bring enormous complexity. And, understanding *what* is happening and indeed *why* it is happening is one of the toughest challenges a crisis leader faces. Indeed, the governor commented with self-effacing modesty (and in reference to a systems thinking concept) that he failed, at the beginning of the 2008 crisis, to identify it as a *prisoner's dilemma*. This is a confession Lord King also makes in his book, *The End of Alchemy: Money, Banking and the Future of Global Economy*, which builds on his experience of the period. He laments not having spotted it sooner.

Leadership deadlock can accompany such dilemmas for the decision maker and it needs to be broken. For Lord King, this was achieved through the British prime minister at the time, Gordon Brown's decision to galvanize the leaders of the G20 group of leading economies, and their central bankers, into a coordinated effort to tackle the crisis. This had the dual benefit of providing both *common and shared purpose* and a platform to fuse together *intellectual firepower*. This, he believes, was a critical decision and a turning point in the crisis.

However, while full of praise for Brown and his counterparts at other central banks, King reserves most of his praise for the young economists at the Bank of England and the role they played in working with him to debate solutions.

For Lord King rigorous *back and forth debates* are utterly essential in decision-making in a crisis to avoid what he refers to as a *quickly found, middle way*. When dealing with the complexity a crisis brings, this might be the easy way to make decisions. But, as he notes, it certainly won't be the most effective. With a twinkle in his eye, he challenges leaders, at moments in which key decisions are made, to surround themselves with people who are not just technically capable, but who are also willing to challenge the leader for the benefit of achieving the common good. It is incumbent on leaders to create an environment in which that is not just acceptable, but expected.

Just before he finished his term at the bank, I watched Lord King interviewed by a renowned British broadcaster who asked him how he coped with the stress of his role during the crisis. In reply, the governor conceded that it was stressful. But, said he had never suffered *real* stress. Real stress, he said, was experienced by people who had lost their jobs and were struggling to make ends meet.

Nevertheless, I was keen to know how he coped with the magnitude of the decisions he was making. His advice was threefold.

First, leaders must know themselves and how they work most effectively. Whenever he had control of his own agenda, mornings were for thinking, reading and writing. Meetings were banished until the afternoon.

Secondly, leaders must constantly remind themselves of the *big picture*. They must delve periodically into the detail. But, they must *raise above it all*, particularly if they are facing criticism, which is inevitable in a crisis.

Thirdly, they must cut down the distractions and consider the long term. Or at least chose them carefully. The governor did not have a *Bloomberg screen* in his office and so avoided the minute-by-minute vacillations of the market. And, he largely avoided the news media. But, he did allow himself to read informed financial commentators to understand how his decisions were being received and the *external narrative*.

But, said the Governor as he elegantly returned cup to saucer, what leaders absolutely must do is wake every morning with their *own* narrative in their heads. They must know what they need to decide that day and what they need to get done. And, with that focus they need to cut through the noise and, quite simply, get on and do it.

5

Crisis team leadership

One of the most compelling moments in a crisis management adviser's professional life is the last step he or she takes towards the room in which the crisis management team is meeting during a live crisis. Sometimes the journey from an organization's reception to the CMT meeting room is inauspicious. It looks, and feels, very similar to the walk to any meeting room on any day of the week. If you didn't know the organization was in crisis, well, you wouldn't know.

Sometimes it is very different. People are rushing around the main floors, and the route to the CMT is blocked or obscured. Security guards occasionally block the path, and you are required to show ID before you are allowed to go any further. Inevitably, this heightens the sense of anticipation.

It doesn't matter how many times I do that journey – nor how many security guards block the way – my blood pressure is always higher. While the atmosphere and what I see around me is interesting, the sense of anticipation relates to my curiosity about what I will find when the door to the CMT meeting swings open. And that can vary – enormously.

At one end of the spectrum, what greets me is noise – and lots of it. Some people cluster together, talking rapidly and over each another. Others are moving around the room, clutching papers and speaking at speed into mobile phones. No one appears to be in control. At the other end of the spectrum I am greeted with an almost cathedral-like hush. There is a controlled sense of urgency in the air. Apart from a couple of people who are writing on wall-mounted boards, most people are sitting and talking. They are making their point while also listening. At the head of the table is the leader, who is quite clearly in control. The confidence such a scene breeds is extraordinary, and my blood pressure lowers as a result. From experience, I know that the crisis is likely to be led effectively, and the path towards a resolution will be less fraught.

This chapter seeks to understand how this confidence is attained. It addresses the crucially important challenge of crisis team leadership.

Let's lay down some theoretical foundations for what we mean

Woven inextricable into the notion of 'crisis team leadership' are dozens of threads. *What is a team? What is effective team leadership?* And, what is 'effective' in this context? The list of aspects that present themselves for potential exploration is innumerable. That's because organizational life is a form of social science which doesn't lend itself easily to analysis. And *teams* are particularly tricksy.

In today's globally connected world, teams work across borders and time zones. However, all teams have to interact, and they have to meet, whether that's virtually or in person. It's during these meetings that the sheer complexity of a 'team' presents itself.

The next time you are in a team meeting, try and rise up above it. Imagine you are watching it via a CCTV camera in the corner of the room. Putting aside the Orwellian overtones, what you will see is a fascinating display of human frailty and flawed interaction. Team interactions can be moments in which years of personal frustration emerge, or platforms for colleagues to momentarily clash, taking their interpersonal rivalries a step further. They are layers upon layers and are as much about what is *not* said as about what *is* said. Or they can be like a stream in an English country meadow. They drift pleasantly along but seem to move with little impetus and even less direction. They don't really *go* anywhere.

The reality is that teams are run badly in 'business as usual' situations. Add in the amplification factors of a crisis and the ineffective behaviours (rarely the effective) are turbocharged. The result is the chaos I have invoked in the first scenario described in the opening paragraphs of the chapter and the outcome is poorly executed crisis management, the blame for which will be placed at the feet of the crisis leader. And, frankly, rightly so.

To avoid this, and get to the desired cathedral hush, we need to get back to the basics and remind ourselves of the building blocks of effective team working. As I have endlessly said, the competencies required in a crisis are enhanced versions of those needed during business as usual; team working and team leadership are no different. That's why I began this chapter with a brief journey through the millions of words that have been dedicated to teams and teamwork by academics, practitioners, industrialists, soldiers and politicians.

I follow this with the very practical steps, I believe, crisis leaders can take to run the CMT in order to ward off the amplification factors that threaten to undermine the effectiveness of the response.

The building blocks of effective teams

I do not intend to commit many words to definitions of a team or teamworking. Let's use American academics Steve W. J. Kozlowski and Bradford S. Bell's definition, which was put forward in their 2003 article 'Work Groups and Teams in Organizations'. They describe teams as:

collectives who exist to perform organizationally relevant tasks, share one or more common goals, interact socially, exhibit task interdependencies, maintain and manage boundaries, and are embedded in an organizational context that sets boundaries, constrains the team, and influences exchanges with other units in the broader entity. (Kozlowski and Bell 2003, p. 334)[1]

This definition serves us well. And I'd like to propose my own definition of team leadership, which is the '*forming, directing and overseeing of a group of people in order to effectively achieve a commonly held and clearly understood goal.*'

I'd rather dedicate more words to the characteristics that make up a successful team. And a number of points here are critical for the crisis leader to remember.

Teams exist within wider, fluid contexts

First, teams do not exist in isolation. They exist, within a series of concentric circles which begin with the environment, contract into the organizational context and end at the team, or the specific *group context*. Secondly, effective team leaders must range across these areas, scanning them for opportunity and for threat. On this, I need to say more.

FIGURE 5.1 *The crisis leader in an environmental, organizational and group context.*

The environmental context

The environmental context is the broader setting in which the CMT operates. It is an environment in which teams from other organizations form to respond to the crisis.

They are the teams from the emergency services, the regulators, perhaps community groups, or specialist contractors or consultants. The crisis leader must therefore be alive to:

- teams which operate entirely separately from the core CMT in the external environment.

- teams which overlap with the CMT. This overlap coming from the provision of supplementary CMT members by teams that are ostensibly separate to it, or from teams which share a similar mission.

For some crisis management experts, a crisis is defined by the need to bring *extraordinary resources* to bear. These extraordinary resources manifest themselves in those teams which are either seperate or overlap with the CMT.

This is a situation that is not materially different from those in which most leaders find themselves in on a daily basis. In contemporary organizational life, teams are rarely staffed purely with full-time employees of the

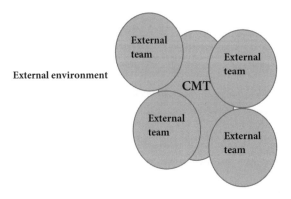

FIGURE 5.2 *The CMT in its operating context.*

leader's organization. Consultants and freelance staff move fluidly across organizational lines.

However, this doesn't come without its challenges in terms of maintaining team cohesion, for example, or in ensuring information is in the correct hands. And, consistent with one of the central themes of this book, the amplification factors of a crisis can greatly magnify such day-to-day challenges. Not least because, in any crisis, CMT leaders may have external members forced upon them by competent authorities, some of whom may have a different view on how the crisis should be responded to.

Even where that is not the case, and teams remain as separate entities, differences of agendas and goals will emerge. What may be a crisis for one team may be an opportunity for another. In other words, the sort of rubs that can exist between individual team members within the CMT can be transposed into a team-level challenge.

General Stanley McChrystal talks about this at length in his book, *Team of Teams*, as he reflects on his team while serving in Afghanistan and on the multiple different teams that were working to fix a common problem but were working in silos. He notes how inefficient this became. His answer is to recognize that the challenges between teams represent those between individual team members, and in response, crisis leaders should forge a *team of teams*.

To achieve this, McChrystal emphasizes the need for a clear, shared and agreed sense of purpose, which helps each team see the interconnectedness of the whole problem. He posits that transparency is often the key to achieving this.

As an aspiration, I entirely agree. It reflects the pursuit of the sort of superrationality that I have touched on in Chapter 4. However, I also recognize that achieving it, particularly in a fast-paced, incident-driven crisis, is far from straightforward. Thus, I counsel leaders to be aware of the potential friction that exists in the external environment and the potential for lost efficiency as teams bump into each other and duplicate efforts. In addition, I counsel leaders do whatever they practically can to shield members of the CMT from such inefficiency. As a first step, it means creating a relationship with the leaders of the other individual teams to assess the appetite for the sort of shared vision that General McChrystal advises, and determine what steps might be taken to achieve it. On some occasions this is achievable. On others it is less feasible. Every situation has its own dynamics.

The organizational context

While teams operate across evermore fluid lines, CMTs are housed within an organization – the one at the centre of a crisis. I will call this the 'home organization'.

It is a constant refrain within the broader team leadership literature that what sits around a team within the home organization must help rather than hinder.

Richard Hackman, former professor at Harvard Business School and one of the most noted scholars on team effectiveness, is a prolific contributor to the debate on what leads to effective team dynamics. In his book 'Why Teams Don't Work', Hackman urges enormous caution when approaching the organizational context surrounding teams (Hackman 1998, p. 27).[2] He believes leaders and managers must ensure their team has the right kind of structure – not necessarily more or less. He recognizes the temptation to instinctively dismantle as much structure around a team as possible, deeming these to be 'bureaucratic impediments to group functioning' (Hackman 1998, p. 252). Yet Hackman stresses it is not the amount of structure that is always the biggest challenge to efficiency, but the *kind* of structure. It must enable and assist the team, instead of making it harder and more complicated.[3] But, what does that mean in real times and in a crisis?

I always counsel crisis leaders seeking to maintain CMT effectiveness to be hyper-vigilant in the home organisation for:

- **Deliberate or accidental dilution of their authority:** Leaders across the organisation may take it upon themselves to unilaterally 'fix the problem' without recourse to the CMT leader.

- **Unacceptable or unreasonable expectation of success:** Members of the home organization are no less susceptible than members of the court of public opinion to demoting something complex to something facile and declaring the answer 'obvious'. There is no need to articulate the demoralizing impact this has on the team. Expectations need to be managed.

- **Bombardment of the CMT for information:** 'There is not enough internal communication' is the one piece of feedback that any leader of any organization anywhere in the world consistently hears in any internal survey of their staff. In a crisis, it increases. And senior leaders (including Board members) are the worst perpetrators of peppering members of the CMT with requests for information.

- **Well-meaning but unhelpful hustling for involvement:** There are times when organizational members seek to deny resources to a crisis management team. If this happens, it's usually during performance – or policy-based crises. In other words, those which sap resources for considerable periods of time. More typically, though, colleagues seek any opportunity to get into the crisis room, using offers of help to cloak a (possibly) morbid desire to be *part of the action*.

The motivation for all of these behaviours can differ. Sometimes those motivations are positive; at other times, sadly, they aren't. Unfortunately, the outcome, to varying degrees, will be the same. The team could easily waste its time dealing with *internal* tensions at precisely the moment they should be focused on the crisis at hand and *external* concerns.

It is the leader's responsibility to scrutinize the organizational context for any of those factors, in order that the home organization incubates the most effective team it can.

The group context

If you talk to most leaders who are having problems with a team, they typically point to 'troublemakers', or to a few individuals who 'simply can't work together'. Indeed, there may be one or more individuals the leader finds 'difficult'. In fact, I'd be surprised if there weren't. The law of averages says that, in any team, there are bound to be colleagues who have different values or approaches to the task in hand.

However, the academic literature has no truck with the claim by any leader that interpersonal relationships are the guilty party in any attempt to investigate why teams are ineffective. Most argue that this is symptom of a more profound problem, rather than a cause and effect in and of itself.

Richard Beckhard, the American organizational theorist, credited with developing the 'GRPI' model of team effectiveness lists four pre-requisites for effective teams: *goals*, *roles* and *responsibilities*, *process*, and *interpersonal skills*.[4]

Most telling for me is research done on the model by Noel Tichy, an American management consultant, as he sought to uncover what conditions played the dominant role in team conflicts. His research found that 80 per cent of conflicts in teams were due to unclear goals. Of the remaining 20 per cent, 80 per cent were due to unclear roles and responsibilities. Only 1 per cent was due to interpersonal conflict.[5]

In fact, establishing a clear goal unites nearly all other prominent theorists writing on the topic of team effectiveness. In *The Five Dysfunctions of a Team*, American writer Patrick Lencioni, agrees.[6] As does Professor Hackman, who lists it as one of the five conditions for successful teams in his influential book *Leading Teams: Setting the Stage for Great Performances*.[7]

This is simultaneously good and bad news. It is wonderful insofar as the definition of a mission and purpose was so fundamental to effective decision-making, and so it serves highly related roles. On the other hand, it is terrible insofar as this is the one category that is so frequently overlooked when I walk into crisis management rooms. I hope I need write no more on this matter.

However, it is still not the complete picture. Other factors matter too. As Professor Hackman noted, a leader can't *force* a team to perform well. He or she can only create the conditions that give it materially better chances of success. In addition to the need for a compelling direction (goal), essential conditions include being a *real team* (shared tasks, boundaries and stable membership), an *enabling structure*, a *supportive context* and *expert coaching*.[8]

Different teamworking experts focus on different things, of course. American computer scientist Alex Pentland believes communication among team members trumps everything else when it comes to team effectiveness.[9]

Most, however, centre on similar themes to those introduced by Richard Beckhard and Professor Richard Hackman, and thus identify a cocktail of both hard and soft operational factors, all of which are crisply summarized by the authors Jon R. Katzenbach and Douglas K. Smith in their book *The Wisdom of Teams: Creating the High-performance Organization*. In it, they beg us not to overlook the 'basics' when it comes to effective teams. For them, these are:

- Is the team in the right size?
- Do members have complementary skills?
- Is the purpose of the team meaningful and well-defined?
- Are there clear, team-orientated goals?
- Does the team have a concrete, agreed approach to working?
- Is there a sense of mutual accountability?[10]

Once again, these together arrive at a single point: it is the basics that really matter. Not just in a crisis, but in every circumstance. The challenge being, of course, that the amplification factors will catch the leader out if he or she fails to address any of the above points. In a business-as-usual context leaders can often get away with effectiveness shortcomings. Not so in a crisis.

This brings us to the leadership itself, the position which lies at the centre of the circles but which works seamlessly across them.

The leadership task

When I am asked to help clients ensure that their senior people are able to lead during a crisis, I have frequently been asked to make sure that their leaders can execute *command and control*. While few would be able to articulate precisely what defines command and control, most mean they want their leader to be able to lead the CMT in the sort of style most typically associated with military leadership. It is leadership which is characterized by an autocratic, authoritarian style.

There is good reason for this. Equivocal and indecisive leadership hardly leads to effective teamworking in business as usual. Richard Hackman, writing in *Leading Teams: Setting the Stage for Great Performances*, argues that managers who are apologetic in exercising their own legitimate authority are making one of the six common mistakes which lead to ineffective teams.[11] Management consultancy Deloitte's 'Human Capital Trends 2016' report has also had a bellyful. The report calls for team leaders to 'rid their minds of sentimental egalitarianism' and 'clamp down on dithering and waffle'.[12]

Common sense surely tells us that decisiveness is required in a crisis. Indeed, the voices for it do grow louder. The authors Dr Daniel Goleman, Richard Boyatzis and Annie McKee list six emotional styles of leadership that are suited to different circumstances, and which leaders ought to be able to adopt under different circumstances. The styles they list range from *visionary, coaching, affiliative, democratic, pace setting* to *commanding*.[13] Predictably, they land on '*commanding*' as being the most appropriate choice of 'style' in a crisis.

This is nothing new. In the 1960s, the psychologist Fred Fiedler put forward the Contingency Model of leadership,[14] with the purpose of indicating what circumstances suited what type of leadership – specifically, either *task-based* or *relationship-based* leadership. He found that 'unstructured problems' (which a crisis unequivocally is) are better suited to *task-based* leadership. But I urge caution here. And lots of it.

Clearly, during a crisis a leader needs a bias towards task-orientated leadership. Stuff needs to be done. That's only common sense. However, that does not mean giving the leader *carte blanche* for self-appointed demagoguery. Sadly, that happens all too often, and can lead to some of the most ineffective leadership I have ever seen.

This ineffectiveness presents itself in innumerable different ways. Yes, it's utterly demoralizing and spirit-crushing for individual team members, just at the moment when the leader needs them to be committed to an *esprit de corps* as fuel through the gruelling hours and days ahead. But that pales into insignificance against the two main causes of concern:

- a failure to generate – as far as is possible – a complete picture of the crisis that has befallen the organization; and

- a licence to invite the *grand dame* of bias into the CMT – groupthink.

As we have seen from my interview with Captain Hawkins, and the lessons learnt in airline safety which ushered in the concept of crew resource management, a failure to listen to situation assessments while dishing out orders means leaders end up attempting to fix the wrong problem. For some leaders the time taken to work out what has happened or is happening is unutterably painful. Some are, it often appears, in danger of bursting in their desire to *do* something. For these leaders, any permission to adopt command and control leadership is like giving bees access to the honey pot.

The second danger is no less serious. Groupthink, which is essentially human beings' almost indomitable desire for unanimity, has been written about endlessly. It was popularized by the social psychologist Irving Janis in 1972, in his famous book *Victims of Groupthink* in which he looked at the contribution of inefficient decision may or foreign potray.[15] The outcome of Groupthink in a crisis is that teams fail to consider the wide range of solutions that may be available to them in tackling the unending number of challenges the crisis will bring. The team becomes unified around a single course of action. Groupthink is typically associated with very high levels of team cohesion. Crisis leaders must, of course, be alive to an overly-bonded team which is too keen to agree with itself. However, Groupthink can also emerge if team members are too afraid to voice their views if they differ from that of the leader (and other team members). For the inexperienced and untrained crisis leader too keen to exert control, this is as big a danger as high levels of team cohesion.

Despite the simplicity (and drama) of the moniker *command and control*, I prefer therefore the concept of 'directive collaboration'.

Preferential leadership style: Directive collaboration

Directive collaboration is, in my view, vital to connect a leader with his or her followers (there is no leadership without followership!), and thus allow, under crisis conditions, a team to be what a team should be. That is creating wholes that are bigger than the sum of their parts, as Amy C. Edmondson, professor of leadership and management at Harvard Business School, so articulately puts it.[16]

And that's because it allows sense-making to happen. This is, as we have seen in Chapter 4, the 'process of creating situation awareness and understanding in situations of high complexity and uncertainty. It is a motivated continuous effort to understand connections (people, places, events) to anticipate trajectories and act effectively.' This is, to my mind, what leading a team during a crisis is all about.

In a somewhat idiosyncratic style, Karl E. Weick offers seven pieces of advice for leaders when they face leading through the inexplicable. These are represented in the acronym SIR COPE: *social, identity, retrospect, cues, ongoing, plausibility, enactment.*[17] However, what underpins all of the steps is his appeal to leaders to, if not revel in, at least settle into the messiness of a crisis, working with the team to move, in Weick's words, from the *superficial* to the *complex* to the *profound* in establishing what the crisis is, but also about how to fix it. He begs us to protect that process and that truth.

However, the leader needs specific guidance on how to do this. And that's what I'd like to do now, as I would like to give crisis leaders practical guidance on how to bring the words written in this chapter to life.

Narrowing in on the first and second CMT meetings. Why?

To do this, I am going to focus on giving very specific guidance on running the first (and to a lesser extent, the second) meeting of the CMT.

On the one hand, such advice is clearly logical. The various skills required of crisis leaders are presented here, as far as is possible, in the chronological order in which they are required. Chairing such a meeting is the next required step. However, on the face of it, to address team leadership in such a narrow context may appear odd. Too tactical perhaps? There is surely a bigger picture to be addressed here which explores the leadership of the organization more broadly and not just that within the CMT. Moreover, surely anyone reading this book ought to be able to chair a meeting?

These challenges are fair and therefore worth addressing. Clearly the responsibility of the crisis leader is to take a broader view. His or her responsibility is to the *whole* organization, even if the CEO and the CMT leaders are not the same person. The wider responsibility to the greater good remains. However, overseeing the implementation of the hour-by-hour, day-by-day managerial tasks that result from the decisions of leadership are, as they are in 'peacetime', delegated – many of them to members of the CMT. It is the crisis leader's responsibility to ensure that, when the CMT members disburse back into the organization, it is not just with a clarity of what is required but also with a genuine confidence in the crisis leadership. Doubts, worries and concerns will soon be identified and, in a cruel game of Chinese whispers, spread throughout the organization to chip away at morale. Getting these early CMT meetings right, could not be more important.

In addition, and perhaps a touch controversially, distressingly few leaders – no matter how experienced they are – run meetings effectively; at least in my experience, regardless of whether it is a crisis setting or not. Meetings drift, and their purpose is often unclear; they are dominated by one or two individuals; and the actions that result from them are at best unclear and at worst contradictory. That leaders can run meetings is, sadly, far from being a given.

In my experience, an increasing number of organizations recognize the importance of this meeting and understand that mastering the ability to run them is crucial. In 2015, Eric Stern wrote a report for the OECD, entitled 'From Warning to Sense-making: Understanding, Identifying and Responding to Strategic Crises'. In it, Stern writes of the importance of being aware, as a leader, of the enabling and constraining aspects of a small group, and how that helps to improve sense-making 'before and during crisis situations'. He goes on to note how leaders can greatly enhance this by fostering organizational and small group cultures and processes conducive to information sharing and critical deliberation (Stern 2015, p. 15).[18] I am therefore delighted that a trend has emerged among crisis management professionals to speak less of the need to prepare leaders to execute 'command and control' but to speak more of the need to help prepare them to 'run the room' by which they mean ensure their leaders are able to effectively run meetings of the crisis management team.

It is to how to 'run the room' that I turn my attention to now.

Running the room

If we are inexperienced at doing something – or if we are nervous, perhaps even afraid – our field of vision tends to become narrower. With a keen, critical eye, this is clear to see. Dancers may fail to use a full stage, artists don't perhaps maximize the full canvas, footballers don't create or open up space on the field; there is a sense that the game is dominating them, rather than vice versa.

It's the same with crisis leaders chairing their first meeting on running the room. Their responsibility is to be trainer, instructor and coach. They need to see the whole 'playing field' and encourage those with whom they are working to see and use it too.

In specific terms for the crisis team leader, this means ensuring that they use:

- the dedicated CMT room

- the wider members of the CMT, and

- the range of simple but powerful tools at their disposal (which could range from maps on the wall to checklists).

The use of these things helps the crisis leader to continue to maximize those two crucial commodities of *time* and *space* that he or she has secured and to which he or she must cleave. But by building on foundations laid in Chapter 4, it adds a third, and that is *structure*.

The importance of structure cannot be overstated. It is vital to secure:

- **Credibility:** From among the apparent chaos of the crisis, the leader's ability to set a direction of travel and pick his or her way through the next steps ensures the CMT believes in his or her ability to lead them through the situation. In addition, it ensures that team members are able to make a:

- **Contribution**: As we have seen, crisis leaders simply cannot respond to the situation alone. They need other members of the CMT. But they will be hamstrung by the frailties of human cognition. A structured approach which ensures that team members feel empowered and are given a platform to speak will bring out the best in each of them. The outcome of these factors is a mutually shared sense of:

- **Confidence:** The leader has confidence in the team and vice versa.

It is therefore, in my experience, *structure* which is pivotal in uniting leadership with followership within the CMT, which thus charts a common path towards initially containing the crisis. And, ultimately resolving it. It's structure therefore that I want to address now in some detail.

Followership: A team of teams

To bring this to life, let's picture a scene. Imagine the worst situation your organization could find itself in. It is a situation of craven complexity which has, at its outer limit, the ability to bring down your organization. Or at the very least, the ability to significantly impede its strategic objectives. You have been told about the situation, you have successfully deployed the initial diagnostic questioning outlined in Chapter 4. And you have battled your resistance to mobilise the CMT. And you are now on your way to the meeting.

There are three aspects that are critical to 'structure' and thus critical to effectiveness.

1. the set-up of the room used by the CMT.

2. the points covered in the meeting; setting your own agenda.

3. what the leader does between meetings.

I examine each in turn.

1. The set up of the room used by the CMT

The environment in which we work matters. Perhaps it shouldn't, but it does. And it's always been that way. The Greeks didn't build the Parthenon for nothing. Nor do companies, large and small, agonize over the apparently smallest details of the 'space' they create for the staff to work in for no reason. From bean bags to meeting pods, plans aren't pored over for months, sometimes years, for no reason. The surroundings in which we work send signals about *what* is expected of us and *how* we are expected to achieve it, giving us tools along the way to help us with both.

The room in which the crisis management team meets is no different. It doesn't need to be grand. Nor do the walls have to be a specific pantone colour. But, in my experience, it must be dedicated to the CMT and the CMT alone. And if the CMT leader is to enter the perfect space from which to run his or her crisis management team, it should contain:

- a table with signs indicating the roles of each functional representative (e.g. legal, communications, HR etc.).

- at each place there needs to be a checklist outlining the key points to remember for each function.

- a series of wall-mounted templates, which can be written on. These
  templates should include boxes into which deconstructed information
  about the situation can be placed. What this includes depends on
  the organization and its likely crises. But without doubt, this should
  include space for the most basic *information (the who, the what, the*
  when, the where and the why), the objectives, a map showing the
  affected area (where relevant) and a space for capturing actions.

To some this may sound dramatic. But, to some it will sound very basic. Surely, oodles of cutting-edge technology ought to be available to the team? Some technology should, yes. But it's a caveated yes.

Video or teleconferencing equipment is a must. And, for those organizations working with remote locations, a satellite phone is undoubtedly helpful. Telephone landlines also have a place as anyone who has suffered mobile phone outages during metropolitan terrorist atrocities will know. And, access to rolling news is helpful.

But, what of the 'software solutions' that exist to help organizations respond to crises? They do exist. And, more appear every year. Surely they should be at the centre of the response? My answer is that to date I haven't found a solution I am convinced by.

The idea of such solutions is, *in principle*, perfectly sound. As its states on the shiny box, such solutions help via cloud technology to share information with other locations, they help us to log information accurately in ways people can read them and so actions are logged for audit and review purposes. All of that is true. But, the practice is different. And, I have yet to see such a solution be used effectively.

The problem is twofold:

- **getting the technology to work.** Failing to fire up and then
  incompetently using software which is rarely used in a situation of

acute stress damages the credibility of the leader and chips away at an *esprit de corps*. It leaves the leader with a further hill to climb. But, much more importantly, it can, in my view:

- **narrow the field of strategic vision**. Such technology allows us to put things in neat boxes. It forces us to write neatly and approach things logically. And, it allows us to tick boxes and *file the report*. But, here's the thing. Crises aren't like that. They are messy and unstructured. We get things wrong and we change our mind. The facilities we use need not only to *allow* that, they need to *encourage* it. Particularly when operating at a strategic level. When watching teams using *technology solutions*, there is always a sense that rather than tackling the problem, we are completing sections of the software. But, we are not returning to them, scribbling them out and reworking them and then doing it all over again. We are working for *it*, rather than *it* working for us. It allows us to stick with Daniel Kahneman's System One thinking.[19] The face validity of a completed section of software allows us, from a cognitive perspective, *off the hook*. And, that is the very last thing that is needed.

I am not arguing that technology is wrong or that there is no place for it in the CMT. On the contrary, I am urging anyone in the business of developing technology that can support the task of the strategic CMT to continue to hunt for a solution. Technology is moving at such an extraordinary pace that who knows what solutions will be available in twelve months from now. And, future generations of leaders for whom technology has played a far more central role in their lives may use it more effectively. I am merely noting that this generation of leaders must treat it with appropriate caution and not allow its neatness to cloud the need for rigorous and in-depth thinking.

And so then it is to a relatively simple backdrop that the team should work. But, this simplicity shouldn't detract from its impact. That impact is symbolic.

It says that the team is about to work in a situation that is different from *business as usual*. However, its impact is also very practical in helping to avoid some of the key cognitive pitfalls that as humans we are susceptible to.

The stage is then set. Now to use it appropriately.

2. The points covered in the meeting: Setting your own agenda

Team leaders need team members who are able to give of their best. That means that they are able to focus on three things; *themselves*, *others* and the *problem* they are trying to fix. If team members are able to focus on those three things that means they are bringing both intellectual heft and the emotional intelligence required to the CMT.

The challenge though is, of course, that team members may not be in a position to deploy both the *EQ* and *IQ* that you as the leader need of them.

The reasons for that are manifold. Some of them will be familiar to the crisis leader:

- they may well be suffering from the emotional hijack as we have discussed in Chapter 3 and thus they may well not be able to engage the *prefrontal cortex* to deal with the disorientating effects of cognitive dissonance

- they may be concerned about their own involvement in the situation and therefore their own liabilities including their legal and professional exposure;

- they may be suffering from a sense of *bereavement*, particularly where fatalities and injuries are involved. I learnt years ago to never underestimate the likelihood of those on the CMT knowing those who may have lost their lives no matter how large the organization and no matter how widespread its operations. It may be either a deep personal friendship or a chance involvement with each other facilitated by the quotidian execution of organizational bureaucracy. It happens, and it affects people.

And, some of the challenges that create barriers to the full engagement will not be known to the leader either at the beginning of the crisis or for the duration of it. These are the *personal challenges* that we all tackle in our lives. *Births, deaths, illnesses, marital breakdowns, family disputes, illnesses, financial problems.* The list of the potential personal challenges any one of the CMT may be facing is endless. None of them stop when the crisis happens. Indeed, some of them may be exacerbated by the increased commitment that the crisis may require.

The impact of all of this on the individual team members is a potential narrowing of focus. First of the three areas of focus to fall away will be the *problem.* Then team members may well lose sight of *others* before finally succumbing – because they are but human beings – to focus on *themselves* alone.

The role of the crisis leader here is to create an environment which enables them to focus on all three aspects – as much as is possible – in as short a time as possible.

As the leader, you ask team members to begin that journey from the moment you enter the room. As you enter, the scene that will greet you, the wall displays, role cards aside, will be team members doing a range of different things. Some will be engaged in telephone calls, some will be punching out emails or text messages and some will be talking to each other or simply reviewing the checklists that sit on the desk in front of them. However, all will notice the leader as he or she walks in. And, this is a critical moment. But why?

Because followers will be watching every movement from you and every element of your body language for clues as to your assessment of the situation. *How bad is it?* This moment has similar characteristics to the one in which you were informed of the crisis in the first place. And, it's a critical milestone.

When followers are asked in future years about your performance, much of the material they will draw upon to describe your performance will be drawn from the first impression you give as you enter the room and what you do next. Putting all preparatory work aside, it is at this moment that members will decide whether they as individuals will feel 'safe' in this environment and that they will throw their weight behind the team – rather than seek to protect themselves in the weeks ahead.

As ever, the leaders must be authentically themselves. I cannot ask any leader to be something that they are not. Nor will I. What I will do is ask them to ensure that on entering the room their body language communicates that they are in charge of themselves and the situation and not vice versa.

In my experience, this is achieved in two ways.

- **The leader's body language communicates the gravity of the situation.** Particularly if deaths are involved. Followers need their leader to care, and to care genuinely. This doesn't require great displays of emotion. Far from it. But, the amygdala can lead to strange outcomes. Smiles or even an odd sense of excitement can be displayed if the leader does not have absolute control over ourselves. There is a moment for humour. But, it's not yet.

- **The leader speaks and moves with a sense of purpose but not at speed.** Again, the amygdala is still being battled. The risk of moving quickly and speaking too quickly is high. The adrenaline may be pumping. Dig deep and control the movements.

The risk of losing control of either of these aspects threatens leadership credibility. If in doubt, overdo it. But, take care of sincerity at all times.

The importance of these opening moments cannot be underestimated. However, nor can the next two elements:

- the use of a structured approach to the meeting. This is the *what*.

- the disciplined behaviour in which the leader holds the meeting. This is the *how*.

Let's examine both individually.

Agenda: The what

This splits into three parts:

- The opening

- The objectives and actions

- The close

And, I address each of these individually too.

1. The opening

Like a conductor walking onto a stage, the leader must unfurl the score and raise his arms.

- Ask everyone to be seated.

- Thank everyone for being there and signpost or paint a picture of how the meeting is going to be run (see following points).

- Ask everyone to introduce themselves by name and indicate the function and/or role they represent at the meeting. And, at this point, if the leader hasn't done it before, ask if there is anything urgent that needs to be attended to immediately.

- Remind everyone of the *mission* of the team and ask them to remember that throughout the rest of the meeting.

- Revisit the situation as it is known: *What* has happened, *Where* has it happened, *when* did it happen and, crucially, *who* has been affected.

- Ask each member of the CMT if they have any question or observations about the situation as it has been outlined.

It is worth pausing at this point to make an observation.

What never ceases to amaze me, is the number of different opinions and views there are on precisely what has happened. (Not least in the contemporary environment, social media will be bringing a cacophony of external 'noise'. Some of which is correct. Most of it not).

This brings me to my second observation. Undertaking this process will feel painful. For at least 50 per cent of those at the table, the sensation they will feel as they work through this will be akin to pain. Should we just get on with it? But, get on with *what?* Daniel Kahneman's Level One thinking is taking charge. And, it mustn't. It is absolutely crucial that everyone is getting on with the same thing. True crises take days, if not weeks, to respond to. The few minutes (which to some may feel like hours) taken to determine this are essential. And, must not be rushed. And, the leader himself must be prepared to hear new information as the crisis is being discussed.

All the time this is being done, the leader must be working with a small group of people in the room whose predetermined role is to ensure that critical information is captured an well charts or logs, gently directing and guiding to make sure that the inaccuracies are corrected.

The leader must also, in my experience, be alive to three other 'types of information' which will, without doubt, emerge during the course of these discussions:

1 **Actions:** irrespective of how many actions have been noted during the initial discussions, more will emerge. These must be captured.

2 **Questions:** in no crisis I have ever been involved in has the CMT known all the information they need to make all the decisions they need to make. Finding the answers will require enquiries of other

teams. This cannot, indeed must not, slow down what can be done. Questions should be captured.

3   **'Stuff'**: this is 'stuff' which the team, thinks may, possibly, have an impact on the response even if they are not sure how. This is, in essence, a form of sense-making. What that 'stuff' is depends entirely on every variable you can conceive of. In my career, this has ranged from the timing of the Muslim celebration of Haaj to trade delegations to the country in which the crisis has happened.

The team is not yet ready to do anything with this information. Nevertheless, it should be captured. The team is though now immersed in the crisis, and each member will be studying the boards, completed as they are for information that pertains to them. It is at this point, and almost certainly not before, that the leader, having seen all the data gathered and having witnessed his team absorb and synthesize it as required, is able to move on to the second part of the meeting.

2. Objectives and actions

It is here that the leader needs to articulate the objectives of the team. As outlined in Chapter 4, these build on the mission. In many ways they add colour to the mission.

In doing this, the leader is actually achieving three crucial tasks. He or she is:

- raising the team out of the details back into the 'big picture'.
- creating decision-making architecture, which can be taken from the room and back into the functions those on the team represent. But, critically, the leader is:
- creating an *esprit de corps* and binding those in the room into a series of targets.

The importance of each of these points cannot be underestimated. The team is a strategic team and must keep an overview; decisions will emerge at each stage of the crisis to which there is no answer. In these situations, the guiding light provided by a commonly agreed set of objectives is therefore crucial. How the leader, therefore, reaches agreement on them becomes critical.

It is unlikely that all team members will agree either on each objective or perhaps on the order.

The nature of a crisis means that is a sensible working assumption. The leader may therefore be required to take a final decision. However, the bias the leader should display in reaching the objectives should be towards proposal and consultation rather than unilateral direction. Effective leaders in this situation use expressions such as, *given what I have heard, may I suggest that our objectives as a team are,* rather than, *our objectives are as follows.* Some leaders will find this hard. However, it is my firmly held view that an ability to do this shows extreme self-confidence. And, more importantly it achieves a greater level of productive teamwork.

Having agreed upon the objectives, the leaders should then work methodically around the table asking each member of the team what, given the objectives that have been agreed, they believe their next actions are to be. The leader's role is to join the dots, arbitrate over disagreements and help avoid duplication of effort.

Again, throughout this process, the leader should still be quietly guiding those responsible for capturing information on the wall. It should be clear and it should be accurate.

Having done this, the second stage of the meeting is complete. And, the jigsaw puzzle is, for now, complete. And, the team can be dismissed. Almost. Before calling the meeting to an end, the leader must close it out. This is not hard. But, it is important.

3. The close out

The close out is critical. And, it requires the leader to:

- **Ensure that everyone's actions are clear.** We are terrible at giving this clarity in business-as-usual meetings. Who is doing what and by when?

- **Thank everyone and set expectations.** This doesn't require a Churchillian rhetorical flourish. But, it does require the leader, briefly, to note that this situation may not be easy, but that clear objectives have been given. And, together the team will do its very best for those who have been affected.

- **Remind everyone to consider sensitively what they write down.** Premature opinions as to cause or ill-placed humour aides no one and may give rise to considerable distress during any investigation during which every written word is discoverable by lawyers.

- **Reassure the team that the leader is available.** Decisions will almost certainly need to be made before the next meeting. The leader is there to relieve the cognitive load. Thus, where he or she can be found is critical. And, finally, the leader should

- **Indicate when the next meeting will be.** And, indeed that good a punctual attendance is expected. The purpose of having all functions represented is to ensure that decisions can be taken with all considerations recognized. The whole team must therefore be present.

Controlled discipline: The how

As we have seen throughout this book, effective crisis leadership is not just about the 'what' it is as much about the 'how'.

There is rarely a discussion around how leadership should be executed without the mention of Jim Collins's book *Good to Great*, and his concept of the Level 5 Leader. The book is exceedingly influential, backed with dogged research of what makes good companies great. In all the Good to Great companies Collins and his team identified, all had a Level 5 Leader at the helm. Jim Collins describes a Level 5 Leader as someone who embodies 'a paradoxical blend of personal humility and professional will'. Such leaders also 'display a compelling modesty, are self-effacing and understated' (Collins 2001, p. 39).

I can't think of a better description of effective leadership in a crisis than one which combines *professional will* (which creates results by having an unwavering resolve, sets standard and assumes responsibility) with *personal humility* (which is modest and never boastful, relies on standards not charisma, challenges company ambition and assigns credit to others).

There is though a part of Jim Collins's book which I think is incredibly important, yet so few people discuss it (or many have forgotten it). In *Good to Great*, Jim Collins interviews Admiral James Stockdale, the highest ranking naval officer to be held prisoner during Vietnam war. During the eight years he was held captive, he undertook various acts of heroism, including self-disfiguration to avoid being used for propaganda purposes.

However, his key offering, and one that I cannot help but think ought to be mandatory reading for all those undertaking crisis leadership, was that when dealing with situations of great adversity, 'you must retain faith that you will prevail in the end *and* you must also confront the most brutal facts of your current reality' (Collins 2001, p. 86). Collins called this the Stockdale Paradox. For Admiral Stockdale, while held captive for eight years, those who were overly optimistic or who did not confront the reality of their situation, died of a broken heart. On the other hand, those who preserved an underlying faith, while also recognizing their current reality, prevailed. The Stockdale Paradox is about coming back from difficulty stronger.[20]

In deference to Admiral Stockdale, I will also add that in my experience, leaders must also commit to:

- **Avoiding indications of blame:** This will come. But, it is manifestly not for discussing in the early days of a crisis.

- **Maintaining discipline:** in specific terms, this means (1) **ensuring that team members are not taking calls during the meeting,** but that they are focused and, in the current parlance of mindfulness, are 'present' and (2) **that only one person is speaking at a time.** Pressures in a crisis include poor behaviour which ranges from a verbal fight for survival to what Nancy Kline refers to as 'queuing to speak'.[21] One of the reasons for asking team members for their contribution, *in turn*, is to remove the concern that some may have that they will not have an opportunity to contribute. A cacophony of voices helps no one. Nor does having team members retreat from the discussion because they are tired of not being heard.

- **Deploy a range of emotions and behaviour but manage impulsive signs of emotion.** If an emotion is required to achieve an outcome, take an active decision to display it, otherwise do not allow it to be displayed. And, humour, used carefully, has its place here too. But, critically.

- **Show that you care.** Time and time again, if I ask team members about what they value in a crisis leader, the answer is that the leader *cares.* In my experience, they nearly always do.

3. What the leader does between meetings?

There are many things that a leader can and should be doing between the first and second and indeed any subsequent meetings of the CMT. They should, for example, ensure that the minutes taken and the actions agreed are noted for subsequent enquiries and reviews. However, what the crisis leader must do is ensure that the team has precisely what he or she worked so hard to secure for themselves; *time and space.*

This means attending to three activities specifically:

1   **Being available for the team.** I won't revisit this in detail. The team
    will face decisions that can't wait and which they can't – or don't want
    to – take by themselves. The leader must be available to assist with this.
    However, just as important is that the leader is:

2   **Talking to senior stakeholders.** Both the leader and the team
    members will be inundated with calls from (well-meaning) senior
    executives. Working through a prepared list, the crisis leader must
    ring around key internal stakeholders. This has the benefit of both
    ensuring that team members spend their time undertaking their
    actions and boosting the credibility of the leader and his team. A
    proactive call is worth one hundred times the most elegant remarks
    made in response to a received call. And, finally, it is important that
    the leader is:

3   **Thinking.** And, howsoever they best wish to do this. To date, the
    crisis leader has reacted to the crisis. And, has undertaken basic
    diagnostics tasks and indeed set the team immediate actions.
    However, in a true crisis – whether a wicked problem or otherwise
    – dilemmas will be presented to the crisis leader which will demand
    high levels of cognitive agility. Now is the moment to begin
    considering how the situation could deteriorate still further. The
    leader is not expected to predict each and every twist and turn.
    That would be an impossible ask. But, like a marathon runner who
    has studied a route in advance of a race, if the leader has already
    contemplated some of the challenges which may lie ahead, he or she
    will tackle them with for greater confidence and aptitude should the
    time come to face them than they might otherwise have done.

In my experience, all of these tasks leave the leader and his or her team as well
placed as they can be to tackle subsequent meetings of the CMT.

Subsequent meetings

Nearly all of the guidance provided for the first meeting is fully and equally applicable to subsequent meetings. All of the structure and discipline has to remain. The *how* doesn't change. Although the *what* may change a bit.

What is true of nearly all crises is that the strategic CMT and its members will, as the situation develops, need to stop dealing with individual actions which sit neatly within individual functions. Rather they will need to slowly deal with 'workstreams' or 'themes' which will require siloed functional thinking to be replaced by longer-term, cross-functional problem solving. What these are depends, of course, entirely on the crisis. They might be *support all those negatively impacted* (in a safety crisis) or *rebuild customer loyalty* (in a policy crisis). The CMT leader may at this point ask functional representatives to lead a 'thematic area' or bring additional subject matter experts into the team. Project managers may be recruited to proved support. The emergence of such workstreams is typically, if not always, evidence that the crisis is moving beyond the initial containment phase. Thus the leader may have more times and space to consider how he or she optimises the approach to tackling the themes or workstreams identifical (while ensuring that the team maintains its momentum and sense of urgency).

Conclusion: Controlled urgency underpinned by a sense of directive collaboration

Some readers may complain that I am teaching them how to run a meeting in this chapter. And they would be right. I am. To an extent at least. And, in my experience, I need to. Many leaders have lost the ability to run effective meetings. In our desire for *transformational* and our rejection of *transactional* leadership, we have ushered in meetings without start, without purpose, which lack structure and drift towards inconclusive ends. There is no place for that in a crisis. I am not proposing a return to the reductionist world of 1950s corporations. I am though advocating an approach which ensures that:

- Everyone speaks their mind.
- Everyone listens
- The crisis is dealt with at its intellectual core and with its impacts in mind.

By following the approach outlined above, give or take the requirement to allow for organization-specific idiosyncrasies, that's what leaders will achieve. Crisis leaders ignore it at their peril.

WHAT MAKES AN EFFECTIVE CRISIS TEAM LEADER?

Lessons from the battlefield: An interview with General Stanley McChrystal

I conducted my interview for this book with General Stanley McChrystal over the telephone. We hadn't met before. But, I knew there would be much to learn from him on leading a team in a crisis. He is, of course, a highly decorated, four-star general in the US Army and he has written a bestselling book which is an accessible study in how teams work.

But, it was a comment made by a member of my team, a former British army officer, about General McChrystal just minutes before my call with him that sealed my belief in how important his contribution to this book would be.

In a bid to usher my colleague out of my office so I could place the call, I explained who I was about to talk to. 'Wow', he said, standing quickly. 'General McChrystal. Now he's a soldier's soldier.'

So, what did a man whose impact had percolated through the ranks of the thousands of troops who had served under him through to my colleague (who had never *directly* served under him) have to say on team leadership in a crisis?

Our discussion began in very general terms. And, the general made two observations which will be familiar to any crisis leader.

They are that at the outset of a crisis, leaders must draw a deep breath and stay doggedly committed to the long term. However, they must note that along the way that they will constantly be sitting on the 'horns of a dilemma'. Become too involved in the detail of the response and leaders are accused of overreaching. 'Step back' and leaders risk being accused of not caring (which is almost never the case). Finding the balance is fiendishly difficult. But, find it they must.

Written in the pages of a book, there is a risk that his words sound weary. Not a bit of it. From the outset of our conversation, the general, who is blessed with an exceedingly warm and reassuring baritone voice, exuded positivity and unbounded enthusiasm for discussion on a topic he has clearly discussed countless times before.

This experience of discussing the topic shines through in the extremely orderly fashion in which he articulates his view on what it takes to run a team in a crisis. For General McChrystal, effectively running a team in a crisis requires crisis leaders to:

1   Understand how their **organization** works and be able to impart
    that knowledge. They need a deep knowledge of their organization's
    fundamental building blocks: its structures, processes and
    approaches. In fact, General McChrystal puts this organisational
    knowledge above *technical* knowledge relating to the specific crisis
    at hand. Leaders, he says, need to share that knowledge with their
    teams in order the teams know how they relate to other parts of the
    organization. And, other teams. They need to know the *connections*.
    Leaders also need to:

2   Understand how **people** work. Leaders need to know how to
    communicate with and how to inspire them.

It is on this second point that General McChrystal expands at length but with elegant precision and, in my experience, rare specificity.

Most people like teams, he explains. They want to be part of teams, and teams form organically. However, to be effective teams need to be small. People, he believes, cannot relate easily to 'big things'. It has to be personal. People want to *matter*. And, if they feel that they do, the leader can harness the very best of their abilities in tackling the crisis at hand.

For General McChrystal, central to achieving this is the mission the team is set. 'Instead of asking a team to undertake a task, I ask them to fix a problem'. Yes, team members do ultimately need to leave a meeting knowing what they need to do. But, by tackling a *problem* rather than a *task* and being tasked to do this 'in broad brush strokes', the team becomes cohesive.

That doesn't mean the leader's role is finished. Far from it. As the team goes about its mission, the leader must demonstrate an ability to *listen* and to *explain*.

Listening is, he says, something that the military values more than, say, the corporate world.

And, he gives useful guidance on how leaders, through simple rules, can encourage that in their teams. Asking, for example, the most junior member of the team to speak first is something he strongly advocates. If a senior officer speaks first, he says, the chances are that the rest may simply agree. In addressing a complex problem (as opposed to attending to tasks) listening plays a vital role in encouraging utterly necessary debate. Unless you engage each and every member of the team the information the leader is working with is incomplete.

However, *explaining* is critical for successful team leadership too. This needs to happen on an individual basis, he says. When the team experiences the sort of setbacks a team operating in a crisis always will, spending time with its key members is critical. 'Don't let them cry on your shoulder. Explain the big picture and remind them what you are trying to achieve. From this they sense they are not alone', advises the general.

But, this is also necessary within the team context. General McChrystal encourages *thinking aloud*. 'The leader should summarize what he or she believes has been said and vocalize the moment at which a decision is about to be made'. This allows team members to correct misunderstandings (which will always occur), raise concerns (which will always be present) and influence the decision right up to the last minute. Listening and explaining combined.

I am not a soldier. I have never been one, nor ever will be. Yet, as a result of my time on the phone with General McChrystal I would unquestionably follow him into battle. I spent some time over a cup of tea after our call, reflecting on how he had earned my loyalty, over the telephone.

And, the answer suddenly struck me. He had, quite simply, done what he advises others to do. He *listened* and he *explained*. Never once did he cut across my question, interrupt me or seek to anticipate what I was about to ask. And, he welcomed and encouraged my questions, routinely prefacing his answers with a comment on the quality of my enquiry or observation and a moment of vocal reflection.

What he had done was, in theory, simple. But, so hard in execution. General McChrystal did it, however, with consummate ease, elegant charm and personable modesty. That's why he receives the ultimate accolade from those team members whose loyalty he needs. That's why he is a soldier's soldier.

6

Crisis leadership in public

If you ask senior executives to tell you what springs to mind when they think of a 'crisis', most will talk about television interviews. And they will almost certainly do so with a grimace on their face. There are few things that provoke such fear in senior organizational leaders than three and a half minutes in front of a camera.

Whether their concern is justified is a valid question. The TV studio (and all it represents) is not the graveyard of executive careers that many fear it to be. Thousands of interviews happen every day of the week around the world, proving that they are indeed survivable. The problem is, of course, that when they go wrong, they can go spectacularly wrong, both personally for the leader and the organization they represent. No one wants to be the next case study in 'how not do it'.

No book on crisis leadership would therefore be complete without addressing this most dreaded challenge. Focusing on television interviews isn't to forget, or underestimate, the challenge of the many other platforms from which a leader might need to communicate during a crisis. These can range from internal 'town hall' meetings to community meetings to government hearings. However, these platforms do not compare to the ubiquitous interrogation of 24/7 news. (Plus, so many of the techniques needed to survive a TV interview intact can be harnessed for these other challenges).

So, for all of those reasons, this chapter busies itself with ensuring that, if you are chosen to sit in front of those pristinely groomed interrogators, you have the skills to emerge with your career intact and your organization's response goals furthered.

Addressing crisis leadership in public in three parts

I tackle this challenge in three distinct parts:

- In the first part, I examine the journey CMTs typically take to field a media spokesperson. In doing so, I examine some of the concepts critically linked to this, such as reputation management and what *communication* can really achieve. And, indeed, what it can't.

- In the second part, I frame the very specific advice that leaders need to take ahead of any media interview, as well as investigate the idea of the *court of public opinion*. This links the organizational concepts such as *reputation management* to the various structural challenges the spokesperson will need to overcome.

- In the third part, I conclude with four preparatory steps that crisis leaders need to take when tackling this most feared of crisis leadership tasks.

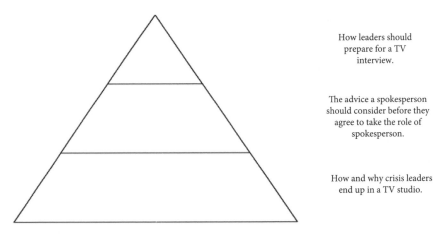

How leaders should prepare for a TV interview.

The advice a spokesperson should consider before they agree to take the role of spokesperson.

How and why crisis leaders end up in a TV studio.

FIGURE 6.1 *Addressing the challenge of the television interview.*

Part one: The journey to the TV studio

The decision to field a broadcast media spokesperson is never taken lightly. Too much is at stake. By the time those feared words 'joining me now to discuss this, is …' are uttered, multiple considerations have been assessed by the organization. So before we get into the nitty-gritty of the preparatory steps which need to be taken by the crisis leader nominated to become the public face of the crisis, it is worth working our way through the steps taken up until that moment and to explore the raft of strategic and tactical considerations that should have been taken. I would like, in effect, to press the pause button before any answer to those so-often-heard words is uttered. And, to press rewind.

Pressing rewind

The steps taken that result in the leader sitting in the TV studio are, in principle, relatively straightforward. They are as follows:

- **Step one:** The **crisis happens.** The organization is thrust for all the wrong reasons into the public spotlight. Or, in an issues-driven crisis, there is significant and growing external comment on the issue;

- **Step two:** As a result, **reputational damage occurs**. This, in simple terms, means negative things are written in newspapers, negative comments are made by commentators and 'experts' on TV news stations, and social media platforms are a whirl of intrigue, rumour and criticism about the organization. Although very unpleasant, that is in and of itself not a bad thing. The enormous problem is that it leads to the following step;

- **Step three:** This negativity leads to **behavioural changes.** Or at least it has the potential to do so. Customers stop buying our products; donors stop donating; voters stop supporting; investors dump shares; banks close credit lines; regulators increase their scrutiny; employees leave (or become demotivated); job applications dry up. These are the direct behavioural changes that cannot continue unchecked. If the crisis and its recovery don't kill the organization, this toxic cocktail of decreased income (or support) and increased costs might. So how can it be stopped? Or, as the question is typically framed within the CMT, how can we minimize the reputational damage of the crisis?[1] To answer this question, all eyes turn to the communication team, which leads us to:

- **Step four: The communication team reviews its approach** as part of the overall response. At this point, it's necessary to stress two points.

First, it is certainly true that the overarching stewardship of an organization's reputation is the responsibility of the communication team or wider corporate affairs department. However, that is true only insofar as the human resources department has responsibility for people. An effectively managed reputation (like an effectively engaged workforce) is the outcome of a collective effort.

Secondly, the communication department cannot undo the crisis. It cannot unspill oil or uncrash a plane, any more than it can uncommit a terrorist atrocity or (alone) make a CEO's strategy work. This may sound obvious, and to an extent it is; however there is often an exaggerated view of what the corporate affairs or communication director (or equivalent) can achieve. He or she cannot make a situation go away, nor can they stop negative media coverage.

What the communication team can do is to support the overall objectives of the CMT by, typically, trying to achieve one of the following:

Guide stakeholders on what to do in order that the crisis is not exacerbated. It is (sometimes) incumbent on the organization to give direction on what customers (or other stakeholders) should do to protect themselves. This is often done in conjunction with a competent responding authority, such as an emergency services or a regulator.

Examples abound from the owners of an oil refinery giving instructions to local communities following a fire, to a consumer goods company providing instructions on a product recall to a technology company advising its users following a data breach. This public information role of communications is often forgotten, but certainly shouldn't be.

Convince stakeholders of the commitment of the organization to the response. Sadly, we live in a world in which it is assumed that, unless pushed to do so, an organization will do nothing to support those who have been impacted by a crisis. In my experience, this is total and utter nonsense. Nevertheless, it doesn't remove the need for the organization to communicate about what it is doing to attend to the problem. This is typically to demonstrate – perhaps contrary to expectation – that the organization has empathy and humanity. But, it is also meant to show that it is doing what it can to minimize the impact howsoever that impact may be felt.

Reassure stakeholders that the crisis is not indicative of a structural failing. Organizational reputation is built on an expectation of performance, in terms of *what* the organization does and *how* it does it. Reputational damage (and, critically, the resulting negative impact) occurs when an organization falls short of that expectation. The communication team is therefore typically trying to communicate and prove that the situation currently being dealt with is either not its fault nor indicative of a deteriorating level of performance.

These objectives are fairly straightforward insofar as they belong in the early containment stages of a crisis and, typically, in the left-hand incident boxes of Griffin's crisis typologies.

The final (possible) objective is altogether more challenging and either belongs much later in the lifecycle of an incident-driven crisis, or is related to the 'right-hand box', performance or policy crises which are more existential in nature. In these, the objective is typically to:

Persuade stakeholders of your view. *Is a CEO's strategy working? Is a firm too leveraged? Will a fraud that has been uncovered have a material impact on the organization's financial performance? Is it ethically acceptable to route revenues via a country with lower corporation tax even if very little business is actually undertaken there?* That the organization has considered the need to defend its position is an indication that it is either in crisis (suffering reputational damage which may influence stakeholder behaviour, which thus threatens its objectives) or perhaps it hasn't succeeded in persuading stakeholders of its position to date. The existential nature of these crises, the fact that personal values drive stakeholders' views – rather than any clear and generally accepted view of what is right or wrong – makes these type of crises materially more difficult for the communication team to tackle. The organization will almost certainly never convince all of its stakeholders of its view.

However, irrespective of the nature of the crisis, the communication team will (or should) approach the task of mitigating reputational damage through communication by identifying:

- **The audiences.** In most crises, the clamour for information comes from a multitude of different stakeholders. The communication team must identify the outcomes it is seeking to achieve (in support of the overarching objectives I have discussed in Chapter 4) and therefore who it needs to communicate with as a priority. The team must then decide on the:

- **The message.** What is said is critical. That, of course, depends entirely on the situation and the desired outcome. And finally, they must decide on:

- **The medium.** Or, in other words, how the message is delivered to the stakeholders identified. And the range of choices here is endless.

From town hall meetings, to social media posts, to press releases, to internal intranet posts. The platform the communication team chooses to deliver the message is almost as powerful as the message itself. And from then on, it is likely that we quickly reach;

Step five. A decision is taken that the best way to deliver a series of messages to a multitude of audiences – in a bid to arrest the behavioural changes that have occurred as a result of reputational damage provoked by the crisis and which threaten the organization's strategic objectives – is to field an organizational spokesperson.

The hunt is then on to determine who should undertake this role. There is no simple answer to that. It is a role that is extremely time consuming and utterly draining. Ideally and if resources allow therefore, it might be undertaken by someone who is not just appropriate for the role – a point I return to later – but also one who is not chairing the CMT . It is often a different crisis leadership role as I outlined in chapter 2. However, whoever takes it should:

- be cognizant of the challenges that are baked into the process of executing it at a societal level.

- have robust answers to a number of specific questions as to why fielding a spokesperson is a sensible idea at all.

Part two: The advice a spokesperson should consider before agreeing to take the role of spokesperson

Throughout this book I have stressed the need for crisis leaders to *frame* the different challenges they face in their wider context. It is so easy to be captured by the amplification factors of a crisis and lose sight of the bigger picture.

However, nowhere is it more important to than when considering a broadcast media interview.

The court of public opinion

During the course of a crisis, most organizations are required to enter two different types of 'court': one is the *court of law* and the other is the *court of public opinion*. It is generally the latter we are dealing with when we consider the leader's position ahead of a broadcast TV interview.

Invoking the concept of a 'court' of public opinion – and in doing so stimulating a comparison with the court of law – isn't perfect. However, it's instructive and I use it to frame the role of the spokesperson.

In broad terms, the purpose of both courts is to uphold a commodity in society that we talk of a lot while underappreciating how utterly imperative it is to everything that we are and everything that we do. That commodity is trust. Trust binds democracy and liberal market economies (and through it every transaction we make), and is a necessary facet of every aspect of our personal lives. It's why we put such importance in the notion of 'reputation' (which is, as noted above, how trust is typically discussed in organizational terms).

A crisis is a moment when that trust is threatened. We trust an airline to fly its aircraft from A to B; we trust an oil company to extract hydrocarbons without spilling them; and we trust a bank to deploy our money safely for our benefit and those of its shareholders until such time as we need it.

When this trust is broken, the courts of law and public opinion – both of which we have developed as societal concepts over thousands of years – work in tandem, and in pursuit of trust's bedfellow, the truth (as it is judged and perceived), to try and determine why and how this failure happened.

No case needs to be made for the power of the court of law. It can impose heavy and direct penalties, bringing with them both direct and indirect costs that can irrevocably impact an organization. Organizations work hard therefore to ensure that they operate within the confines of the laws that apply in the jurisdictions in which they work.

However, the power of the court of public opinion looms, no less large. In a society that permits free speech, the court of public opinion demands a certain set of standards. The fear of finding ourselves at the wrong end of negative social media comments, politician's ire, non-governmental campaign groups' attentions or negative media reporting is very real.

It is thus an all-powerful, unseen but omnipresent regulator without portfolio, playing an indirect but key role alongside the court of law to ensure that the food we eat is safe, the drugs we use are effective and the politicians we elect aren't corrupt.

Thus when that trust is threatened because a gap emerges between what is expected and what actually happens, this court swings into action, noisily voicing its concerns, demanding 'the truth' and reassurances of containment. If our response, via a media spokesperson among other measures, fails to satisfy the court, reputational damage ensues, the result of which is the sort of direct costs the CMT is trying to avoid.

This is all admittedly somewhat theoretical. But considering and keeping it front of mind should help spokespeople rememberduring the hard slog of a crisis that.

- **This is not personal.** They are a small cog in a civic wheel. It's part of a social construct we have created (and from which we live prosperous lives).

- **It will end.** The civic wheel will roll forward. Although the attention will be unwelcome and seemingly endless, it will come to an end.

With that in mind, it's necessary to narrow in on the very specific skills spokespeople will need. And to do that I will remain with our analogy of the courts of public opinion and law, but will examine the differences between them rather than the similarities.

How the courts of law and public opinion differ

The differences between the two courts during a crisis are manifold. But, in framing what the crisis leader has to do, I will focus on four:

First, the passage of time between the moment a court of law is opened and when the court of public opinion commences proceedings is vastly different. Lawyers have huge tracts of time to collect evidence, build their cases and huge opportunity to weave their arguments into an elegantly constructed proposition, which can be delivered with aplomb over a huge period of time. The court of public opinion (often) opens the instant an (incident-driven) crisis has begun. The defendant is asked to take the stand without delay and has, perhaps, three and a half minutes to make their case.

Second, the court of public opinion lacks a judge. The problems this creates are numerous, but the most critical of them is that the media itself steps into the legal vacuum. At an abstract and theoretical level, this ought not to be a problem. The media, after all, controls the (virtual) court room, by which I mean the airwaves (and the column inches for newspapers). However, the media assumes the role not just of judge but also of attorney for the defence, or indeed, and more usually, the prosecution. This leads us quickly to perhaps the most critical difference, which is that:

Third, the burden of proof lies with the defence, and not the prosecution. From the rise of political populism around the world to the rise of anti-capitalist movements, the concepts which are represented by the organizations most likely to find themselves in the court of public opinion – be they corporates representing capitalism or political parties representing democracy – are most likely to enter the court of public opinion with the presumptive finding of 'guilty'. This is in stark contrast to most justice systems, which are built on the basis of innocent until proven guilty. Whether this is right or wrong, or merely a cyclical period in which systems have 'winners' and 'losers' baked into them as concepts, is a question for a different book.

Admiral Stockdale would no doubt encourage us to simply accept the brutal facts of the matter, which are explained by Ken Stern, the former CEO of America's National Public Radio (and formerly a lawyer) who wrote in *Vanity Fair* on 3 November 2016:

> In a fragmenting media world, with rapidly changing norms and vast choices for consumers, any media company that wants to survive over the long run, will need to factor in the demands of their best customers for news that fits their political biases. That need not be done by changing the facts, as happens too often in many places online, but by offering stories that cement a particular view of the world.[2]

All of which leads to a big decision for both communication team and leader, because:

Fourth, we are not compelled to take the witness stand. In a court of law which has a judge, the accused or witnesses can be compelled to take the stand. In the court of public opinion, no such rule applies. Quite apart from the fact that this adds, in general terms, to yet another decision which has to be made by the CMT, a huge amount of judgement is required as to whether your spokesperson should take the stand or not. But why?

Making a decision as to whether your spokesperson should take the stand in the court of public opinion is not the same as making a decision as to whether you are on trial or not. That decision lies with news editors who consider stories collected by journalists, be they staff or 'citizen journalists'. Clearly, if the situation is significant enough for the organization responding to it to consider it a crisis, then it is self-evidently 'news worthy'. Not only that, if the court has opened, the need to fill air time means that dozens of experts will be invited to give their view. None of whom can be guaranteed to know the specifics, but all of whom can be guaranteed to have a self-serving reason to give evidence. Those reasons can range from self-promotion through to a desire to see the organization in the dock suffer maximum reputational damage.

The question then becomes: is it better – despite the structural challenges inherent in the differences between the court of law and court of public opinion – to field a spokesperson to put across the organization's point of view?

The answer to that, in theoretical terms, is yes. Crisis communication experts are united in the advice that every organization should do everything it can to 'own the story'. Michael Regester and Judy Larkin wrote 'tell it all, tell it fast, tell it truthfully' (Regester and Larkin 2008, p. 218).[3]

Steven Fink, in his 2002 book *Crisis Management, Planning For the Inevitable*, notes: 'If the media can communicate the news the instant it happens, crisis communications dictate that a company *must* be prepared to respond almost as fast. The inability to communicate your message skilfully during a crisis can prove fatal. And it would be a totally needless demise, a wrongful death' (Fink 2002, p. 92).[4]

This, of course, not only presents the 'court' with arguments for the defence, but it meets that unfathomable need during a crisis for humans to see another human face.

This advice has survived, in principle, the two most recent revolutions in the court of public opinion, namely the advent of 24/7 news and our internet-enabled reliance on *citizen journalism*.

It is, however, only a starting point as a piece of advice. To take it at face value would be naive in the extreme. The advice must be considered with caveats, and lots of them.

The necessary caveats

While the variables are endless, in my experience the communication team must satisfy themselves – and satisfy the spokesperson they propose fielding – that despite the possible volume of interview 'bids' being received and no matter how much pressure the CMT is under to 'minimise the reputational damage', they can answer the following very specific questions with an unequivocal 'yes'.

Are we sure we won't make the reputational damage worse by fielding a spokesperson? This isn't about shying away from responsibility, hiding or ignoring the best advice. On the contrary. There are times when not commenting or drawing attention to the situation is, if the strategic objectives are to be achieved, the most effective thing to do. Examples aren't hard to find. There is, for example, little to be gained if your organization sits far down the supply chain and, while it has mobilized a Crisis Management Team, is not being called on to lead the public response. This position may change over the lifecycle of the crisis. But, a judgement is required at each step. Nor does it mean that we don't provide written statements. But, there is a difference of intensity between providing a written statement and spokesperson. Equally, if a regulatory body or government department is involved in the crisis response, they may lean heavily on an affected organisation to *not* field a spokesperson.

Is it appropriate for us to respond? This question ought to be answered, to an extent at least, through the clarity I have urged (in Chapter 4) the CMT to have in defining the organization's mission. It is typically about appropriateness and is a query often raised when the emergency services are involved. For example, an explosion at a petrochemical plant will, almost certainly, require the operator (or owner) to field a spokesperson. However, the local community will want to hear from the local emergency services. And they may wish to hear from them as the most prominent spokesperson, particularly on issues related to safety or public health.

Will the appropriate spokesperson be able to demonstrate sympathy for the victims? In my experience, there are very few leaders who do not feel deep and genuine sympathy for anyone affected by the crisis that has befallen their organization. With vanishingly few exceptions, leaders don't become leaders without a deep sense of humanity. However, feeling deep sympathy and being able to communicate it effectively are two different things. Some people are, quite simply, better at it than others. Whoever is chosen has to be able to communicate their compassion.

Is our message better delivered via the main stream or social media? Before the social media age, the only way of reaching a mass audience in a very short space of time was via broadcast media. In theory, this has changed with the advent and wide availability of YouTube and other platforms. But, YouTube followers, for example, typically reach interested (positively or negatively) smaller segments who are therefore likely to be your advocate or enemy, irrespective of what you say. Thus, to reach a broader range of people, or those who may wish to see us being held to account, agreeing to be interviewed on a national or international broadcast network may indeed be the most effective communication route to support our overall objectives. However, one particular question should be posed.

Do we have enough information? Any situation in which all of the information required to solve the problem was available would, by the definition I have proposed at the beginning of this book, fail to be classified as a crisis. Therefore, in the same way that a lack of information cannot be a barrier to decision-making, nor can it be a barrier to refusing to field a spokesperson in the court of public opinion. However, elegant judgement and careful consideration are required. If the world is clamouring for a spokesperson, but, the spokesperson might – through a lack of information – be at risk of making the situation worse and/or themselves look foolish or incompetent, then the organization should probably stand behind a written statement. This question is, in my experience, one of the hardest to answer.

Can we reach agreement with the legal team? In any characterization of any CMT, the legal team wages a pitched battle with their communication colleagues. In this stereotype, the legal team considers the communication team to be naive and too quick to say 'sorry' (for everything). The communication team believes the legal team to be emotionless with an inability to see the 'bigger picture' and thus uncommercial. I exaggerate for the purpose of effect. And, truth be told, the lines have been less firmly drawn in recent years. Nevertheless, stereotypes exist for a reason, and it is not hard to work out why. In contrast to the communication team's bias in a crisis, which, as we have seen, is to 'tell it all, tell it fast, tell it truthfully' (Regester and Larkin 2008, p. 218), is the legal team's usual preference, which is to 'say nothing, do nothing and admit nothing'. The challenge is that they both approach the situation from a departmental rather than an organizational perspective. The answer typically lies somewhere in the middle of these two views.

Is there an outlet or programme that will reach the audiences that we wish to reach but will give us a fair hearing? No broadcast network is without a programme or interviewer known for their aggressive and unbending style. Someone who is watched less because of their pursuit of the 'truth' but rather because the sport of watching them attempt to unseat a (possibly) well-meaning interviewee in the process is entertaining. With the odds often so heavily stacked against anyone who takes the stand anyway, it's hard to argue that accepting an interview bid from such an outlet is a sensible course of action. As a result, an outlet or platform which gives us a fair hearing – or an approximation of one – has to be a prerequisite.

The court of public opinion is a ferocious place, and only becoming more so. That doesn't mean that we shouldn't have a bias towards 'taking the stand'. This advice is decades old and remains as relevant today as it has always been. However, this is should be done only where the communication team and spokesperson can reconcile to the caveats above. If they can and the decision is made, then the spokesperson must embark on a thoughtful but essential series of steps to prepare to ensure that they can meet this most public of tests head on.

Part three: How crisis leaders should prepare for TV interviews

There are, in my experience, four steps crisis leaders should take to prepare for broadcast interviews. These are centred around ensuring that the spokesperson knows:

1   **what they want to achieve**

2   **what they want to say**

3   **how they are going to say it**

4   **how to behave in front of the camera**

Its necessary to explore each.

Know what you are trying to achieve

I am a big believer that far too infrequently in organizational life, in whatever we are doing, do we ask the question: 'What we trying to achieve?' And that's in peacetime, when perhaps the biggest threat faced is a benign loss of momentum or focus. In a crisis, the need for discipline is, of course, far greater.

Earlier in the Chapter I have provided some very broad objectives as to what the communication team might be trying to achieve in a crisis. However, I want to give some generic advice that is relevant to the spokesperson and indeed relevant to most crises.

The first step the spokesperson needs to take ahead of any interview is to ensure that they know, with as much precision as possible, the audience they are communicating with. In other words, who are the viewers?

Clearly, if the interview is with a national broadcaster or perhaps an internationally known network, then the audience may be familiar to the spokesperson. However, in most incident-driven crises, communication teams will, in addition to major national broadcasters, try and agree to interviews with smaller, localized outlets to communicate perhaps with local audiences. These may be less familiar.

The most important point here is that far too many spokespeople confuse *medium* and *audience*. They believe the medium (the interviewer) is their audience and that is not the case. The *viewers* are the audience. The more effectively the spokesperson can visualize their audience, the greater will be their ability to communicate with them. Powerful spokespeople work, in effect, *around* their interviewer. To do that they must be able to picture the right audience.

Once the spokesperson has done this, they must satisfy themselves that they know what they are trying to achieve in communicating with the audience.

My suggestion is to try and consider it from the perspective of what it is we want our audience to: *know, do* or *feel.* There isn't really anything else that communication can achieve. Clearly, the specifics of what one is trying to achieve depends on the individual requirements of the specific crisis. However, it's possible to make some general comments on these as goals. For example, it's easy to articulate what you want your audience to *know* or *do* (even if there has been disagreement on what that ought to be). Both lead themselves to a level of specificity.

Making your audience *feel* something is altogether more intangible. While is not impossible, it's also much harder to prove that you have achieved it (unlike measuring what has been 'done'). Nevertheless, trying to leave your audiences *reassured* or *confident* or *impressed* is no less a critical organizational objective.

To conclude this brief section though, I would urge any spokesperson to try and avoid any temptation – or proposal – that involves trying to engender sympathy, either for oneself personally or for the organization during a crisis. Any attempt by a spokesperson to engender empathy by identifying themselves as a victim should be avoided. This can require enormous emotional intelligence.

That doesn't mean a company shouldn't try to defend itself, or say 'sorry', or even remind the world that at the root of a crisis might be an attack by terrorists or nefarious criminals in, say, a data breach crisis. However, in nearly all cases, this mustn't cross the line to become an appeal for sympathy.

Know what you want to say (and what you don't want to say)

Politicians have unwillingly given the art of media television interviewing a bad name. Endless interviews see politicians chased around in a verbal game designed to make them say something they just don't want to say. The thrill is in the chase. This has been studied in depth by the psychologist Dr Peter Bull. He analysed thirty-three British televised political interviews and found that the average direct reply rate of politicians was only 46 per cent.[5]

And it doesn't just happen in the TV studio. Prime Minister's Questions, displayed weekly in the British parliament, is a superb form of verbal jousting which serves up a mind-blowing array of skills and techniques.

While this may, at one level, be tremendous fun for the audience, it can leave a sour taste and has left many organizational spokespeople sceptical about the need to prepare for interviews. I have worked with so many spokespeople, both in live crises and as part of crisis preparedness planning, who arrive with the notion that 'I, unlike others [sic], am going to tell it how it is'.

This is not wrong, it's laudable. No spokesperson should ever lie. Nor, indeed, does anyone want them to be evasive. An effective spokesperson is someone who is believable and credible, and not trying crassly to avoid the question. The spokesperson must try and close the gap between themselves and their audience.

However, the problem lies in another gap, the one that lies between what the spokesperson wants to say and what the interviewer wants him or her to say. The two may not represent polar extremes, but they may also not be aligned. The spokesperson wishes to achieve an objective, but the interviewer wants, in his or her role as prosecutor, something different. Sadly, this can, at times, be to demonstrate that big business or politics is, inherently, *bad*.

To manage this, the spokesperson needs a set – usually three – of what are typically referred to as *key messages*. Put simply, key messages summarize in a sentence or two what it is that the spokesperson wishes to say to his audiences.

These messages serve two purposes. They:

- **ensure that the spokesperson is focused on what it is that he or she wants say (in order to achieve his objectives).** The interviewer may wish to roam far and wide in their questions. For the spokesperson to achieve his or her objectives, he or she must know what he or she wants to talk about. Critically, he or she must also know what they don't want to talk about. Thus, they also;

- **provide the spokesperson with a place of safety.** They can be returned to as topics should they find themselves being pushed to respond to questions which can't yet be answered.

But what should these 'messages' be. Surely, they are crisis-specific? Yes, of course. However, in my experience there are few better places to start than the 'crisis messages' first proposed back in 2005 by Michael Regester and Judy Larkin:

1 **Care and concern:** for the people and the environment that have been affected.

2 **Control:** over the situation. (And, in addition, I have latterly added *containment*).

3 **Commitment:** to the investigation and ensuring that, whatever has happened, it cannot happen again, in so far as that is possible.[6]

These 'messages', although in perpetual need of refinement, work well. They work for situations that are highly emotive and involve mass loss of life, and indeed those which pose a less emotional reaction.

There are, however, two important observations to make about these messages:

1   **The formulation of the words that are used to articulate them has to be authentic to the individual leader.** There are occasions when the formulation of a 'message' is very precise. There is a requirement or a desire to use a very specific set of words. Generally though communicating a message is about communicating a broad sentiment. It is critical here that the spokesperson chooses the words he or she uses carefully. Two leaders may use a slightly different set of words to communicate the sentiment. What works for one will not work for another. The leaders themselves are not often able to judge this for themselves. An advisor is often required to help select the words he or she uses to effectively communicate the desired sentiment.

2   **The formulation of the message must be strategically consistent and robust.** The spokesperson's message must reflect the response strategy and must be able to withstand scrutiny.

This second point requires further comment. Many people consider the notion of communicating with the world directly (via social media) or indirectly (via the media) as being a modern phenomenon.

Nonsense. Engaging with 'publics' is the art of rhetoric. It has been around since the dawn of time and can be traced through biblical references, and is of course something the Greeks busied themselves with understanding. Aristotle provides us with a way of thinking about it, which is as relevant today as it was in 400 BC, that messages are based around and built upon a mixture of what he referred to as *logos, ethos and pathos.* As Sam Leith simply describes, in his popular book on the topic, rhetoric is simply 'the art of persuasion: the attempt by one human being to influence another in words' (Leith 2011, p. 1).[7]

To discuss this further, let us return to our court room metaphor. In both courts, a position or a view is unlikely to be accepted without *proof* or *evidence*.

Let's take as an example the crisis leader who is representing a technology company whose service has suffered a catastrophic shut down. The more the crisis leader can describe the very specific steps the company has made and the progress it has achieved in rectifying the problem the better. This is an example of Aristotle's logos.

It is hard to overstate the important of logos. The details must exist. This is, in fact, where the communications and the overall response must work in harmony. It is hard to say we have the situation under control, or even that we aspire to do so, when there is very little *tangible evidence* to suggest that we do. With the lawyer for the prosecution in the court of public opinion keen to press home (the confirmation bias) that the organization is 'doing nothing', the spokesperson is on shaky ground if he has nothing to prove the very specific steps that are being taken.

It is here, therefore, that most senior communication professionals would seek to influence the operational response to ensure that the spokesperson entered the court of public opinion with his defence intact.

However, we are appealing equally to the hearts and minds in the court of public opinion, and thus there is a requirement for Aristotle's pathos and ethos. And it is here that battles are so often won or lost. The crisis leader might tell us of how many years' experience both he and his colleagues are drawing on to attend to the problem (and thus draw on ethos). Or, he might, metaphorically, take us into his organization by painting a picture of the number of people working around the clock and who will 'not stop until the impact of the crisis is reduced' (and thus introduce pathos).

The overarching point here is that the spokesperson must be focused, and he must have messages to provide that focus. Those messages must be proven and be evidence-based with both hard and soft proof. They need to be rich and have bite. They need to be compelling if they are to accomplish what they need to achieve.

However, no interviewee is going to be allowed to simply repeat their messages. For that, choose a YouTube channel. In a media interview, spokespeople need mechanisms to help them deliver their message effectively, sometimes under very aggressive questioning.

Know how you are going to say it

Ahead of any interview, it clearly makes sense for any spokesperson to consider as many of the potential questions as possible. However, it simply isn't possible to prepare for every single permutation of every single question. There are simply too many of them. Plus, the questions are, in any case, likely to be driven, at least in part, by the other news items of the day.

The crisis leader therefore needs to be able to spot potentially dangerous enquiry typologies. Hearing any question posed within these formulations ought to ring immediate alarm bells.

In addition, however, spokespeople must be skilled in the art of using the 'bridging technique'. This technique, despite being revealed with great grandeur during media training sessions, is, on paper, as easy as ABC. On receipt of the question, the interviewee:

- either *Answers* the question or when doing that is clearly not possible (because it is one of multiple traps that can be laid), the spokesperson *Acknowledges* the question.

- After which he/she *Bridges* away using one of the multitude of 'bridging phrases' available, and attempts to

- *Communicate* one of the three key messages available to him/her.

It is, of course, the bridging technique that has become so synonymous with the accusation that politicians are 'not answering the question'. To that I would make a number of points in defence of the bridging technique, for the benefit of those crisis leaders from other walks of life:

1 **Organization spokespeople are not politicians.** Politicians are treated differently to most organizational spokespeople. As that most famous of British interviewers, Jeremy Paxman, notes in his book, *The Political Animal: An Anatomy*, 'There is – or ought to be – a natural

tension between reporters and politicians' (Paxman 2007, p. 2).[8] In their defence, there are multiple reasons a politician may be unwilling or unable to give details (proof points) on how a particularly policy position (a key message) may be implemented. The result is a lively and sometimes entertaining verbal tussle between interviewer and politician. Other spokespeople are unlikely to be treated in the same way, at least not in the early stages of a crisis.

2　**It can work for both interviewer and interviewee.** It is (sadly) true that the objectives of the interviewee (uninterrupted delivery of their messages) and the interviewer (an organizational scalp and an interview which becomes notorious for it) often lie at opposite ends of the spectrum. But there lies common ground in the middle. The interviewee wants to deliver their messages in a fluid and authentic fashion; the interviewer wants to conduct an interview that produces answers that the audience find interesting. The use of the bridging technique can help both parties to achieve that, not least as it stops the interviewee becoming a stammering wreck with nothing to say and unable to answer (the sometimes) unanswerable questions put to them.

3　**The rules of engagement mean the alternative is worse.** Let's take speculation as an example. If you take a look at this morning's newspapers or listen carefully to the questions posed by interviewers in most interviews, they will nearly always focus on an unknown future. 'What would have happened if, let's assume X....' etc. Let's put this into a crisis context and you are, say, a pharmaceutical company executive appearing on an international news network to discuss the global recall of a bestselling drug.

No matter how early in the process, the interviewer will ask how the product could have been contaminated. It may be months before you will know for sure. The investigation may involve dozens of organizations and many hundreds of people. Yet the question will come, 'How could this have happened?' A well-prepared spokesperson will know, certainly during the containment phase to close this down, referring perhaps to the investigation that is ongoing. The reason for that is that the alternative is worse.

Let's assume for a second that the spokesperson has, for a while, explored with the interviewer one of the very many potential explanations. These range from deliberate product contamination through to a production line fault. And from there we explain briefly whether other products could have been contaminated, and over what sort of time period. And thus how many patients could have been infected.

Very soon, media outlets around the world are dominated by an apocalyptic picture of corporate genocide on an unprecedented scale. What's the outcome? Healthcare professionals are in chaos as patients start to question lifesaving drugs, patients stop taking drugs they are prescribed, the company share price has fallen through the floor and the spokesperson has, most likely, lost their job. And rightly so.

By exploring the options and telling it how it is, they have not changed the status quo and in doing so undertaken a noble act on behalf of society. What they have done is, potentially, create mass panic.

And so, with Admiral Stockdale by our side, we simply accept that the use of the bridging technique, no matter how much we would love to hate it and no matter how much we may dislike it, is a necessary evil. Avoiding it is the fastest way to appear in the gallery of case studies we are trying so hard to avoid.

There is one final point to raise in the delivery of an interview and that is the use of our old ally – space. I return to this in order to raise two points.

First, one of the most significant dangers of the bridging technique is that the interviewee gets stuck, returning to the same message. By doing this, the interviewee may not be damaging his or her own career or indeed causing the organization any damage. But they are failing to maximize the opportunity presented by the interview.

The use of the full range of messages available creates space and interest and will help the interviewee minimize the chances of getting caught in a rhetorical dead end by the interviewer; more importantly, however, it will maximize the chances of achieving the key objectives.

Second, an effective interviewee often has to manage the space, creating it and gently closing it down in a fluid and barely noticeable fashion. At the heart of this lies an appreciation of the need for certain asymmetry in both the question and answer.

If the question posed is very narrow – for example, what is the flight history (of the plane which has crashed) – the interviewee may seek to answer the question specifically as a form of acknowledgement but then pull the answer back to a more general high-level message about the importance of safety at the firm. If the question is broad, perhaps too broad (which can happen, particularly with a lack of preparation) and is, for example, 'how could this have happened', the interviewee is advised to 'ground' the answer. For example, 'we don't know, but what we do know is that we fly x flights per week, our fleet is one of the youngest and this particular plane had....'

All of which is to say that an interview, like well-written prose or an elegantly constructed opera, has highs and lows, light and shade. It has a certain rhythm to it. And an experienced and well-rehearsed spokesperson will be able to *feel* their way through it. It's when that sense of feeling is lost, the bridging technique becomes rigid and, sadly, the objectives remain far from achieved.

All of this takes practice. And confidence, of course. Anyone who thinks otherwise is, I am afraid, neither nobler nor wiser. They are simply wrong.

However, no matter how clear his or her messages and no matter how well they are delivered via the bridging technique, all will be lost if the interviewee doesn't know how to behave in front of a camera. And this is the final bit of the jigsaw puzzle.

Know how to behave in front of a camera

Meeting in someone else's office is always less comfortable than meeting them in your own. There is always a sense that the host has the slight upper hand. And indeed they do; familiarity breeds confidence. That is why difficult meetings are typically held on neutral territory. This is, naturally, relevant when it comes to considering broadcast media interviews.

It is, of course, possible that broadcast interviews are undertaken in the spokesperson's office (or office building) or indeed at the scene of an incident-driven crisis. To an extent this can be negotiated by the communication teams (depending on the dynamics of the day).

However, wherever the interview takes place, there will be cameras, there will be a camera technician, (possibly also a producer) and the interviewer, who may be someone you recognize. In a studio, all of this unfamiliarity is, of course, exacerbated by the presence of a 'set' and the strange sense of urgency which pervades.

As a spokesperson, it is highly unlikely that you would not be accompanied to the interview. Your adviser will therefore help you to remember so many of the small, but critical things you must not forget, from turning your phone off to not making off-the-cuff remarks ahead of the interview.

However, there is a moment after which you are on your own and no minder can help you. And when acting as an adviser in these circumstances, there are ten things I find myself typically reminding clients about as we chat before they enter the studio alone.

Know how to behave on TV

1 **If you have chance, ask what the first question will be**. They will tell you. But don't be put off by a change in the interviewer's demeanour once 'on air'. Their relaxed and friendly style will suddenly become intense and professional and less personal. The performance, for that is what it is, has begun.

2 **Sit with your bottom firmly in the back of the chair,** sitting on the back of your jacket (if you are wearing one) and lean forward into the question trying to keep as still as you can.

3 **Find a spot on the interviewer's face and keep your eyes focused there** (although be careful not to follow their eyes down if they are looking down at notes). Avoid any temptation to look into the camera lens[9] or to gaze around the room.

4 **Give a brief nod of acknowledgement when your name is given** (but don't use your interviewer's first name). During the interview, avoid nodding as the question is put to you to avoid any sense of tacit agreement with the point the interviewer is making. You may well not agree with it.

5 **Keep your hands clasped in front of you but gesticulate periodically** during the interview for emphasis. Move any further energy into your facial expression to support your key messages.

6 **Whatever the first question, try to use it as an opportunity (after a brief acknowledgement of it)** to deliver all your messages in a structured fashion.

7 **Throughout the interview, pause before you answer** and have a destination (e.g. a key message) in mind before answering.

8 **Speak slowly and in plain language,** avoiding organizational jargon and technical speak at all times.

9   **If you lose your way, or make a mistake, just head for a message**.

10   **Assume the camera is on you at all times** and, after being thanked at the end of the interview, count to three before you move anywhere or smile (or perhaps grimace) because the interrogation is over.

It all sounds so simple. And, on paper, it is. But the execution of it is anything but simple. However, if as a spokesperson you are able to remember the above points, the chances of you delivering your key messages in an effective way that supports the overall objectives, then you will have successfully tackled one of the most challenging and terrifying tasks required of a 'crisis leader'.

In conclusion

The three-minute television interview is a challenge faced by many crisis leaders which generates enormous stress, which in turn prompts huge emotion and in turn therefore devours vast amounts of crisis leaders' energies. And for good reason. There are innumerable considerations to ponder before agreeing to undertake such an interview and countless things to remember while taking part in one. No one is under any illusion as to just how long the impact of something which, in isolation, lasts such a short period of time can be felt if the encounter is not handled with exquisite care. This is why it is, where possible, a role which needs to be separated from the task of running the CMT. Undertaking both roles is often, quite simply, too great a strain for one leader.

However, whether the role has been separated or not, it is to the management of that strain that I turn in Chapter 7. This is not about the role of the leader in public but about the role of the crisis leader in private.

7

Crisis leadership in private

Always bear in mind that your own resolution to succeed is more important than any other one thing.
ABRAHAM LINCOLN 1855

Abraham Lincoln, Winston Churchill, Mahatma Gandhi and Nelson Mandela. Organizational leaders asked to name great leaders would, almost certainly, include these names (among others). And, rightly so. All achieved extraordinary but very different things on their path to a place in history.

However, they are *more* than leaders. They are, for so many people and by anyone's definition, heroes. And they achieve this status by the one aspect that unites their very diverse achievements: they triumphed in the face of enormous adversity.

This is, of course, what a crisis leader must do. They must turn what, at times, seems like an insurmountable task into something that can, pragmatically and in good time, be deemed to have been responded to at worst effectively and at best successfully.

Some perspective is, of course, required. Very few leaders have to lead through crises that threaten global peace. Mercifully, even fewer will ever have to face actual physical torture. Nevertheless, the pressure and stress that crisis leaders go through can seem at times intolerable and can stretch their psychological well-being and personal relationships to breaking point. How can organizational leaders cope with what for many of them will be an unprecedented, once-in-a-lifetime level of pressure? How can they approach crisis leadership in private?

That's the question I address in this chapter. I offer some guidance on how leaders can cope, drawing on the growing area of research that has become known as resilient leadership. And I supplement that with my own advice for crisis leaders based on first-hand experience of the coping mechanisms I have seen deployed.

However, I begin by examining why I believe crisis leaders are so often reluctant to seek coping mechanisms and why their followers (and indeed their wider stakeholders, both internal and external) can often be reluctant to appreciate their need for it.

The maturing of leadership theory

A great number of leadership theories have, of course, emerged over the many years it has been studied. And every period of its study has added an ever-more sophisticated level of analysis and reflection.

Contemporary study into leadership begins in the mid-nineteenth century with Great Man Theory, popularized by Scottish philosopher, Thomas Carlyle. This promoted the view that leaders are born and not made. Great Man Theory is heavily associated with the Carlyle's 1841 book *On Heroes, Hero-Worship and the Heroic in History*. This study of heroes paved the way for his claim that 'the history of the world is but the biography of great men' (Carlyle 1841, p. 127).[1]

Fast-forward a century and Trait Theory takes centre stage. This posits that leaders are born with certain traits that, alone or in combination with each other, will help them to excel in leadership roles.

While far from perfect, Trait Theory paved the way for the behavioural theories of the 1940s and 1950s, which examined less the *traits* leaders were born with but rather more the *behaviours* they demonstrated. This was, of course, a significant moment. It ushered in the acceptance to the claim that effective leaders were made and not born.

From there came a range of what became known as contingency theories, which centred on the belief that there is no single style of leadership that is effective. Rather, certain circumstances require different styles of leadership. The most famous of these contingency theories is Paul Hersey and Ken Blanchard's theory of *situational leadership*, which they developed in the 1960s, and promotes the belief that different situations require different styles of leadership.[2]

That these developments are to be welcomed is, of course, abundantly clear. A glance around the world at the depth of diversity among the leadership ranks of large and significant companies, charities, multilateral bodies and political parties shows that leadership effectiveness comes in all shapes and sizes.

And this book is, arguably, a clarion call of support for contingency theory. I argue that effective crisis leadership doesn't require anything superhuman. Far from it. It merely requires leaders to demonstrate the leadership competencies that they execute every day (e.g. situation analysis, decision-making, communication etc.), with advice on the sorts of behaviours they should exhibit while undertaking them in a crisis in order that they can battle the headwinds of the amplification factors.

That said, I don't advocate a style that would fit neatly into Hersey and Blanchard's four boxes (*telling, selling, participating* or *delegating*). Rather, I advocate a fluid mix of them all. Nor do I particularly advocate the sort of leadership style that might be associated with *charismatic leadership*, which typically centres around leaders with what is considered to be great verbal eloquence and who are able to arouse a very deep emotional response in their followers. (Nor do I particularly celebrate those who are deemed, by whatever definition is used, to be *charismatic*).

There is a simple reason for that. It's not that some of the behaviours typically associated with charismatic leadership are not valuable in a crisis. On the contrary, some of them are baked into the style I advocate. However, such leaders can, in my experience, also be far more prone to the sort of *centralization of control* that I urged crisis leaders to avoid in Chapters 3 and 5, in contrast to those leaders who can call on more some of the more participative behaviours I believe to be necessary.

Yet for all this maturity of thought and much deeper level of reflection, there remains a belief, in my experience, in many organizations that leaders ought to be able to manage huge stress and triumph over adversity, all without the use of coping mechanisms or acknowledging the very great harm it can do to them as individuals – or indeed the great impairment it can be to the efficacy of their leadership.

Is this merely a stubborn hangover from the crass, old fashion and narrow-mindedly masculine view of leaders and leadership outlined above? Perhaps. There are self-evident links. But there is also a danger that we confuse symptom and cause. There is a risk that we miss the fact that this notion of *greatness* and its link with triumph over adversity is, in fact, much more deeply rooted than these (relatively) contemporary theoretical notions of leadership.

The Heroic Leadership Dynamic (HLD)

To prevail over a set of circumstances that are seemingly unassailable is a narrative that humankind has clung to since the dawn of time. It is woven into the very fabric of what we are. The major monotheistic religions, classical mythology, folklore as well as poets and writers through the ages document the lives of those who have triumphed when all appeared lost or give us colourful characters who have battled the odds and won.

The fact is that we need heroes and their grim tenacity in battling the odds. As American academics Scott T. Allison and George R. Goethals, who have written for many years about what they refer to as the Heroic

Leadership Dynamic (HLD) note, hero stories fulfil two human functions: the *epistemic function* (the desire for knowledge) and the *energizing function* (which inspires). And so they have been part of our lives since the concept of storytelling itself began.[3]

And not much has changed. Tales of heroism permeate our lives, from the education we receive at school through to Hollywood's formulaic 'underdog' movies.

All of this influences the views that followers have of leaders, and leaders have of themselves. And that is why crisis leaders are often reluctant to seek the support I believe they need, in order to ensure that they are operating at peak performance.

Real life is neither myth nor disaster movie. The moments when the scale of events threaten to engulf the crisis leader personally can occur when sitting alone, late at night, in the grim half-light of the strip lighting in their corporation's nominated crisis management room, surrounded by the pizza boxes and detritus of (real) humans operating under immense pressure. Or when they are jarred awake in a (faceless) hotel and the grim reality of yet another day beckons. It is at moments like these that our 'heroes', real or fictional, seem very far away.

In these circumstances, it is unlikely to be visions of Moses leading his people through the Red Sea, nor the perfect use of a rhetorical device by Churchill, which will give them the strength they need to continue. Rather the reserves of strength that crisis leaders need to draw upon come from more prosaic sources than that. They come from themselves and the close family and friends who surround them. (As indeed it did for those (real) heroes we all aspire to be emulate when they suffered their moments of despair, which of course, they had too.)

So it's essential in a book on crisis leadership to outline some of the coping mechanisms to which crisis leaders might turn. To do that, I turn first to the research into resilient leadership.

Resilient leadership

As the field of positive psychology grows, so too does the interest in *resilient leadership* or the strengths which enable individuals to flourish. Rashimah Rajah and Richard D. Arvey note that the growing interest in identifying who will 'survive and thrive in turbulent times' was spurred by events like the 2008 financial crisis, and wars in the Middle East (Rajah and Arvey, 2013, p. 161).[4]

But what is *resilience*? According to the American Psychological Association, resilience is 'the process of adapting well in the face of adversity, trauma, tragedy, threats or significant sources of stress' (APA 2014).[5] Identifiable characteristics of someone who is resilient are having an easy temperament, an internal locus of control, a positive identity and being achievement-orientated.[6]

A resilient leader is, therefore, someone who exhibits all of these characteristics. He or she is, simply, someone who doesn't 'break' under trying circumstances.

A hunt through the writing on resilient leadership reveals that it is something we are all capable of. Iris HeavyRunner called resilience: 'the natural, human capacity to navigate life well. It is something every human being has – wisdom, common sense … . The key is learning how to utilize innate resilience, which is the birthright of every human being' (HeavyRunner and Marshall 2003, p. 14).[7]

Moreover, advice on how to harness 'our innate capacity for well-being' is also provided (HeavyRunner and Morris, 1997, p. 2).

Glenn E. Richardson, in his extensive work *The metatheory of resilience and resiliency*, for example, encourages us to *look for the silver lining in difficult situations, participate in positive self-talk* and *meditate*.[8]

In *Helping group members develop resilience*, Rajah and Arvey cite an advisory firm study when they outline a range of behaviours, most of which are associated with transformational leadership,[9] when they encourage *making personal connection, building important relationships, interacting face to face when possible, being open, transparent and authentic and acting on feedback* and *delivering results* as central resilient leadership behaviours (Rajah and Arvey 2013, p. 162).

None of this is particularly unhelpful. However, it is all rather generic. And I have seen a number of very practical and specific coping mechanisms that have helped leaders cope with crisis leadership in private, a summary of which I provide here.

Managing crisis leadership in private: Seven tips from experience

Before I outline these coping mechanisms, it's important to note that what works for one person may not necessarily work for another. Leaders need to decide for themselves what approach or combination of approaches they want to take to ensure that they achieve resilient leadership in the face of, at times, overwhelming adversity.

Learn not to expect either sympathy or praise. Recognize that the media, politicians and regulators are just doing their job and furthering their careers

In Chapter 6 I talked about the importance of not trying to illicit sympathy from audiences or trying to promote empathy by suggesting that, as a large organization or as a wealthy or powerful individual, you are suffering in the same way as others.

However, crisis leaders must go further than resisting any urge to illicit sympathy. They must try and control thier natural need for it.

However, resisting this isn't easy.

Most leaders accept that at least some of the people they lead will criticize them. Followers always know [sic] that they can do their leader's job more effectively. A leader who cannot muster the resilience to know that this is what followers often believe simply shouldn't take a leadership position. However, leading in a crisis under the full force of a relentless counterfactual and possibly highly personal comments about you, all of it in public, is a different order of magnitude and can have a profound effect on the leader. Under these conditions, it is hard to not to experience the sort of emotional hijack I discussed in Chapter 3.

Crisis leaders must resist. They must remember first and foremost that a community of noisy external critics will voice their fury almost irrespective of the crisis leader's actions. The media has content to produce, politicians have to seek publicity which shows them acting in the best interests of the electorate (being the David to their Goliath, in another heroic triumph over adversity tale) and regulators (who typically demonstrate more restraint) must prove they haven't allowed any poor practices to develop which may have contributed to the crisis.

In short, *your* crisis is *their* opportunity. And what's more, they are actually playing a valuable societal role. When an influential commentator calls for a response plan far sooner than one could ever reasonable be developed, they are speeding up the process to resolution.

I am not counselling that this 'noise' should be ignored, nor that influential 'stakeholders' should not be reassured. However, crisis leaders must remind themselves that some stakeholders will always criticize them, and should avoid allowing it to cloud their psychological resilience and cognitive defences.

During a crisis act (and post) as if everything you say or do is going to be public. And, ensure that your family is aware of this too

While the above advice is sound, crisis leaders must also be careful not to inadvertently exacerbate their situation.

As I have outlined above, sustained acute stress has innumerable consequences and leaders must therefore seek mechanisms which provide relief and an escape. However, they must choose a form of release which is not contradictory to the message that either they or their organization is communicating externally. Leaders need to view the world through the eyes of those who are suffering and ask the question, what would the victims expect of me now? Always err on the side of caution.

Of course, in the age of social media and camera phones, the chances of being spotted in an expensive restaurant or enjoying perceived frivolities are exponentially higher. A pragmatic but heightened sense of awareness is utterly necessary.

These all sound so obvious with benefit of hindsight. Yet it's not impossible to conceive how leaders misjudge such situations. In organizations of high complexity, there is always a reason that leaders could be working or returning from leave. Innumerable examples can be found of crisis leaders who have undertaken expensive hobbies as a release from the intolerable pressure or taken a misjudged decision to not return from holiday. They are used to having to resist calls for their immediate return. But, in a crisis, a highly attuned sense of judgement is required.

Sympathy is necessary but don't confuse it with advice

Sympathy is different to advice. And counsel is not the same as altruism.

Everyone needs some sympathy. A difficult day in the office can be soothed by a warm embrace, a tilted head and an opportunity to offload the worries and concerns of the day. In a crisis that need is significantly magnified. And such moments should be taken. But spouses, siblings, parents, offspring wider family and friends will, of course, (nearly) always be biased towards telling you what you *want* to hear, rather than what you *ought* to hear. In doing this, they blur the line between advice and sympathy. Crisis leaders must be alive to this and be disciplined in separating sympathy from advice.

That isn't to say though that leaders do not need counsel in a personal capacity, which may lie outside the organization. Organizational advisers can be captured by their own commercial needs. (litigators want to litigate, communicators communicate; it's what they do.)

Personal friends with professionally relevant experience, who can be relied upon to serve up some brutal facts but with altruistic motives, often provide a useful counterweight to both the captured advice and the well-meaning (and necessary) sympathy.

Warn your family that you will be distracted and unable to manage the quotidian activities of family life

While sympathy runs deep, it does have its limits. No matter how much sympathy family and friends may have for the demands being placed on the leader, spouses don't stop needing each other and children don't stop requiring parents. The danger of a crisis is that poorly managed family life brings a further level of dissonance for the leader. External criticism of their professional life, combined with a growing sense of failure at home, is a toxic spiral that leads to ever-decreasing performance in both spheres of life.

The solutions to this differ and depend unendingly on the nature of the family unit and the layers of shared experiences and coping mechanisms it uses to get through the challenges of everyday life. Crisis leaders who are able to do this effectively typically manage their family's expectations early and not after a series of failed attempts to continue operating as usual. Many adopt a number of mutually agreed rules, ranging from mobile phones off at the dinner table to the taking of children to school at least once a week (during long-running crises).

It isn't my place to guide on the specifics. However, I urge crisis leaders to address this challenge earlier rather than later, so as to remove the potential for every increasing amounts of dissonance and self-criticism.

Don't be afraid to use lawyers. Or at least to consult them

It is in the realm of family that crisis leaders should, with careful judgement, not shy away from the use of lawyers to protect their privacy. If it's necessary.

The crisis leader should expect, of course, unpleasant things to be written and said. But any individual has a right to a certain amount of personal privacy, and the leader's family certainly has.

The social media landscape alone remains hard to police, of course. At a time of crisis (or heightened public interest), leaders should ensure privacy settings are in place on social media, and family members should be counselled to do the same.

However, for content used in traditional media, guidance is enshrined in law and editorial policy typically centred around the requirement for content that is used to be 'in the public interest'.

In a vitriolic world in which social media drives traditional media to push boundaries to the limit, many attempts may be made to push such a line ever further. As a consequence, there may be a need to consult legal guidance in the event that content is used that the leader believes crosses a line.

Taking legal action rarely comes without risks. For example, under UK law, if a crisis leader seeks an injunction, which prevents a story being used by a national newspaper, the media cannot name the party in the injunction. However, if the injunction is unsuccessful because a judge who hears the application deems the information to indeed be in the public interest, then not only is the media free to publish the disputed content, but it can also note that an injunction was sought, a move which invariably makes the content of even greater interest than it may otherwise have been. (Whatever the outcome, there is also the not insignificant issue of the legal costs which are incurred. However, in my experience, these are typically borne by the organization.)

As in every element of a crisis, sound judgement is required. However, a tempered and well considered use of lawyers can be both necessary and effective.

Knowing when it's time to go. This is either because of the values you possess, or because you have a duty to yourself

In Chapter 8, I tackle the notion of ending crisis leadership. As part of that, I deal with how an organization changes or reshuffles its leadership in bid to signal to the world that the crisis is behind it.

If, as part of this, the crisis leader is forced to leave the organization – no matter how that might be positioned externally – then, by my strict definitions laid out in Chapter 1, whatever may be considered to be successful or effective crisis leadership has not been achieved.

There are, however, a number of reasons why the leader may have decided to leave of their own volition, and this must therefore be treated somewhat differently.

In my experience, such a decision is taken, typically, for one or more of three reasons:

1 The cause of the crisis – or the response to it – is at odds with the values of the crisis leader. **The leader steps down (or resigns on a point of principle).** Related to this, but nevertheless different, is the next point.

2 The barriers put up by the organization – or those by the wider stakeholder community – drive the crisis leader to the conclusion

that they are unable to conceive or execute a competent response. **The leader resigns to protect his or her own personal reputation.**

3   The stress of the response is too much to bear, and the leader has 'choked'. **The leader resigns to maintain his or her own physiological and psychological well-being.**

All three serve up profound challenges of judgement. In all cases, the leader will *feel* it more than they will *know* it. That is not to undermine these as sound reasons to step aside, either from the role as crisis leader or away from the organization completely.

However, in each case, meaningful assessment is hard. While crises move swiftly, there are times when they feel endless.

The crisis leader should therefore seek to create the time and the space for their organization and for themselves to assess this situation. In doing so, it's imperative that:

- **They seek the counsel of others**. Both those who are involved in the crisis and those who are not, remembering though to consult those who offer genuinely impartial guidance and

- **This decision is made not on impulse or following a particularly gruelling day or challenging meeting**. Instead, it should be done over a period of days.

When making the decision, though, they must remember one final piece of counsel.

Careers can be rebuilt

Crises can, of course, break careers. Organizational history is littered with leaders whose careers have stalled or even apparently failed because of a crisis which has engulfed their organization or themselves personally. This can happen either because they caused the crisis – either perceptually or in reality – or because they, apparently, failed to lead their organization effectively in the response.

However, for every example, of a 'failed' career, there will be at least one that can be provided to show that, despite what, in the heat of the moment, seemed like overwhelming odds, careers *can* be rebuilt.

This is not to suggest that it may not take time. Nor is it to suggest that careers of a slightly different nature may beckon by design – aspirations can so often change as result of crisis. Our view of success can change.

However, rebuilding something very similar is also far from unachievable.

So, while, I cannot counsel that leaders look to classical biblical or literary figures for inspiration at the darkest moments of their careers, they can and should remember the tenacious triumph over the odds of these somewhat more prosaic examples.

The point is that time, even in these most personal circumstances, is the most valuable and quixotic of commodities. To put it quite simply, time heals. Patience is the virtue required to give it the space to do so.

Conclusion

There is a moment whenever I get on an aeroplane which always makes a big impression on me. It's the moment when the cabin crew remind us what to do in the event of a depressurization of the cabin. Their instructions are clear. They tell us that oxygen masks will automatically be deployed and that we should put on our own masks before helping dependents with theirs.

This seems, somehow, so unnatural. And it certainly isn't the behaviour in the heroic mould. Yet, it is, of course, entirely logical. It may take us a short while to wrestle an oxygen mask onto child, say. During this time, we may be become incapacitated and thus unable to help that the child thereafter. Yet, it will take us a split second to don our own mask and thus leave us perfectly positioned to help our dependents who will need us to be in the best possible condition to help.

And the same is true for crisis leaders. For some, the overarching motivation during their period as crisis leader will be one of self-preservation (or a platform for narcissistic self-promotion). But most care deeply for those who follow them; they wouldn't be leaders in contemporary organizations if they didn't. And, in my experience, they typically dismiss the need to care for their own well-being too quickly. But think about that airborne guidance. The best way to help others in a moment of crisis is, periodically, to look after yourself. When it comes to effective crisis leadership in private, my advice is: don that mask, metaphorical though it may be.

8

When crisis leadership ends

This chapter deals with one of the most vexing challenges that a crisis leader has to attend to and that is ending crisis leadership. These are the tasks required in dismantling the structures of the response and returning their organization to something approximating 'normal'.

Before I get into the intricacies of this, I want to begin by asking you to pick up a newspaper. Or steer your web browser to a news site of a serious nature and review the news items posted today. Whatever your preference.

I am willing to bet that as you drift through the pages you will happen on a story that references or perhaps is entirely about a 'crisis' that has long since dropped from the front pages and (perhaps as a consequence) has long since dropped from your consciousness.

It might be something positive. It might be an observation from an analyst or influential commentator that a specific achievement, possibly a product launch or a set of financial results or an election win, 'signals an organisation's return following the crisis that struck it ...'.

It might, on the other hand, be far less positive. It could be the announcement of the end of an investigation with dire warnings given at a sombre press conference. Or it could be the start of yet another investigation. It might even be the start of criminal proceedings or the sentencing which concludes them.

The point I am making here is though not about what it is that is referenced or what the article is about. The observation I am making and the one I would like you to reflect on throughout this chapter is the sheer length of time that has passed between the moment the crisis referenced was on the front page (analogue or digital) in the full glare of the public spotlight and now.

The chances are that it is not just weeks or months, it is years later. Not infrequently it is decades later. The after-effects of a crisis pervade long after the news media has lost interest.

And, this is, of course, not to forget the very many years the psychological and emotional impact will pervade for the crisis leader. To be clear, I am not suggesting the pain that they may feel is equivalent to, say, that felt by families of those who have lost loved ones or whose communities have been irrevocably changed. Nevertheless, crisis leaders are human. Irrespective of where the burden of blame is ultimately placed, their involvement in an event in which people's lives are affected, is enough to have a lifelong impact on them.

However, while the after-effects of a crisis may continue for so very long, the tasks a crisis leader must execute naturally change as the organization passes the peak of its response to the crisis and interest in that response begins to wane. Specifically, the crisis leader must attend to three tasks which are associated with the concept of ending crisis leadership and these are:

1   standing down the crisis management team and the extraordinary resources required to respond to the crisis;

2   bridging and signalling to (external) stakeholders that the organization believes the crisis is over or has moved to a new phase; and

3   putting the organization on a robust footing for the future.

Each of these tasks – which are, of course, interrelated and interdependent – has to be managed with exquisite judgement. And, I examine each in detail. However, before I tackle the question of *how* they should be tackled, I need to frame the challenge by addressing the vexed question of *when* they should tackled.

Who gets to 'call time' on a crisis?

If we go back to the general definitions of a crisis that I addressed in Chapter 1, then it might be possible to provide some theoretical indications of when a crisis is or might deemed to be 'over'. And, therefore, perhaps straight forward to decide when to commence any of the three activities I outline above. It might, for example, be possible to say that a crisis is over when:

- the threat to the viability of the organization has diminished or the obstacles which prevent it from achieving its mission have been removed. Or, similarly, it might be possible to argue that the crisis is over when

- the amplification factors have started to dim.

Both of these suggestions, however, highlight the fact that crises don't end abruptly. They move through phases and, if we take the time to think in detail about what I propose above, lots of intricate complexity becomes apparent. And that's true for crises across the typological framework I have used throughout this book.

Let's take, for example, a safety crisis. If a plane suffers a catastrophic crash, that specific aeroplane, self-evidently, cannot fly again. However, it is very possible that the cause of the crash may not have been removed. Therefore the possibility of other crashes cannot be ruled out. Thus, the cause of the crisis must be examined as quickly as possible. And, should the cause, be it technical deficiencies or human error, be found to be one that may impact other aircraft, then action must be taken. The conclusions of each step may not be clear cut and may not be undertaken swiftly. Plus, each of these steps requires huge resources and, naturally, leadership. Crisis leadership changes, but it hasn't ended.

The other crisis typologies are arguably even harder to determine in terms of their different phases.

Security crises seem more straightforward, but in fact can be much more complicated. In a cyber-related security breach, the information for which a crisis leader is desperate for is the news that, for example, the loss of data has been stemmed, or at least that it has been ring-fenced. Such an update moves the crisis team forward. Such a confirmation may come. It may not.

Those crises which fall into the governance and performance category are more challenging still. When does a period of financial distress or the impact of accusations of executive impropriety or incompetence 'end'?

To help consider this, there is no harm in looking at the work of some of the academics who have tried to bring some logic to all of this.

Steven Fink, in his 2002 book, *Crisis Management: Planning for the Inevitable*, suggests that crises develop over four stages. These are the: *prodromal* (the warning stage), *acute crisis* (what he refers to as 'the point of no return'), *chronic crisis* (this is also a *period of recovery, self-analysis, self-doubt* and *healing*) and finally the *crisis resolution* phase.[1]

Writing in 2008, Wooten and James suggest that a crisis has five phases (1. *signal detection*, 2. *prevention and preparation*, 3. *containment and damage limitation*, 4. *recovery and damage limitation*, and 5. *reflection and learning*). They helpfully propose the responsibilities of the crisis leader in each phase.[2]

There is no doubting the usefulness of this. Anything that brings logic and sense to such a complex and opaque moment in organizational life is to be welcomed.

But this is somewhat abstract. And, as we have seen, crises don't work like that. Through missteps and miscalculation, they can spin through various phases, and also within the phases as Fink notes in Figure 8.1. In considering these complexities, the crisis leader can and indeed must consult with the wider leadership. In large organizations in which the role of the CMT leader and the CEO, for example, have been separated, the CMT leader should certainly not execute any of the tasks without consulting the CEO and the wider group of executives. Agreement and consensus when reaching such big milestones is utterly necessary not least as the CEO (or even Chair of the Board) may wish to front some of the 'bridging and signalling' activities I will go on to explore even if they haven't been the organizational spokesperson to date.

However, miscalculations can easily develop as the crisis leader tackles three key dissonances, which in my experience typically confuse the crisis

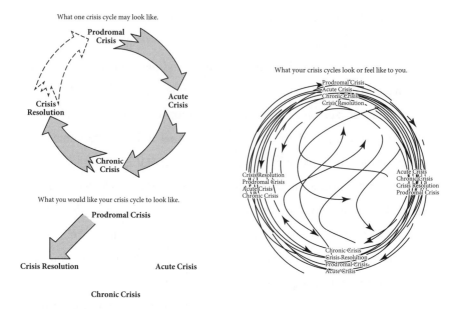

Figure 8.1 *What a crisis looks like versus what it feels like.*[3]

leader (and anyone he or she consults) as to when to fire the starting pistol on the three activities typically associated with ending crisis leadership.

Those dissonances have three sources and come from:

- the leader;
- the responding organization; and
- the many external stakeholders involved.

These dissonances need to be recognized for what they are and tackled carefully and appropriately.

Personal dissonance

The first dissonance is the inner voices that come from within crisis leaders themselves.

Human beings typically find it both tiring and disconcerting to experience any changes in the state or norm to which they have become accustomed. We are ultimately creatures of habit.

But a crisis is change like no other. It brings with it the dizzying stress of the amplification factors and an array of counterfactuals, the sum total of which can, over a sustained period of time, inflict very real psychological and physiological damage.

The outcome of the desire to *end* the crisis (while at the same time recognizing that it may not be *over*) can be the re-emergence of the defence mechanisms I have explored in Chapters 3 and 4. These can swing into action on behalf of the leader and pressurize the leader into executing one of the three tasks too early. Despite what I claimed was an impressive start, George W. Bush's infamous 'Mission Accomplished' speech following the invasion of Iraq is perhaps one of the most famous examples of a crisis being declared 'over' prematurely. It is a crisis which continues to this day and shows no sign of ending.

This is not always the case. I have known leaders who find a greater sense of *self-actualization*[3] when operating under crisis conditions. Rather than wanting to bring the situation to an end, they seek reasons that are nearly always very personal to themselves to elongate the use of the structures that have been put in place to respond to the crisis.

This is potentially less damaging than declaring a crisis over prematurely. However, it can further exacerbate the problem associated with the next source of dissonance – that which comes from inside the responding organization.

Organizational dissonance

In Chapter 7 I note for some experts that a crisis is a situation which requires extraordinary resources to be brought to bear. What those resources are will depend, of course, entirely on the nature of the crisis in question.

However, whether the crisis demands the reallocation of scarce personnel, capital or equipment, resources are being diverted from what many in the organization would deem to be 'normal' activities.

In my experience, two key factors are invaluable to the crisis leader in ensuring that such scarce resources are (re-)directed in the opening hours and days of a crisis. First, predefined and pre-agreed protocols which are collectively developed and collectively agreed, which allow such reallocation. Second, a tight culture which prompts colleagues to help each other (supported inevitably by humanity's unending and wonderful desire to help itself, certainly when death or devastation is caused).

However, such cooperation can disappear quickly. Without much warning, the crisis leader can face pressure to collapse whatever mechanism of response has been deployed and direct resources to the tasks to which they would be typically employed.

This tends to occur when:

- **External public scrutiny has died down.** The impact that a reduction in external media, political and regulatory scrutiny can have on the internal perception of the scale of the crisis never ceases to amaze me.

- **Energy levels have been sapped.** Long days set against a backdrop of the amplification factors can cause a collective of influential or senior people to also want it over.

- **Parts of the organization only indirectly affected become unable to function normally.** For a situation to be declared an organizational crisis does not mean that it directly affects every department, function or location. A situation involving just one product line, say, can be severe enough to mobilize crisis response mechanisms, which can in turn drain expertise and resources from product or service areas not directly involved. Slowly those functions begin to operate less effectively. When combined with the above factors, frustration about this can grow, and calls for the resources to be reinstated will inevitably become louder.

This final point is a clear demonstration of why this internal dissonance is not an altogether unhealthy tension. The rapid containment of the situation is a primary goal of the crisis leader. However, one of the leader's roles is to ensure that resources are assigned to ensure that the rest of the organisation runs smoothly, even if some resources are temporarily redeployed.

Crisis leadership is not being effectively executed if, in response to the crisis, the poor allocation of resources itself becomes a barrier to the organization undertaking its mission. In such cases, the response is creating a crisis in and of itself. This organizational pressure is possibly to be cautiously welcomed.

However, such a welcome should not be extended if it is driven not by the needs of the organization, but rather by professional self-interest or poor or deliberately narrow-minded interpretations of the continued impact of the situation on a range of different stakeholders.

This brings me to my third and final source of dissonance: that which emanates from external stakeholders.

External stakeholder dissonance

The task of categorizing and then managing *stakeholders* is no simple business. It's a job that all organizations have to do, but few do it to their own satisfaction. It's not hard to establish a reason why. Creating lists of stakeholders and, as

Permanently Negatively Affected

Temporarily Negatively Affected   **(Temporarily) positively affected**

FIGURE 8.2 *A way for crisis leaders to consider different stakeholder perspectives.*

most organizations are inclined to do, putting them into boxes to help consider how they should be engaged is, in principle, easy. The problem is that, rather annoyingly, stakeholders are people who demonstrate a frustrating fluidity in their criticality to the organization, their views on it and with whom from within it they want a relationship.

The sad reality therefore is that most tasks require a different and bespoke way of understanding the stakeholder universe. Crises are no different. The model I frequently turn to, outlined in Figure 8.2, when working with crisis leaders to understand external stakeholder dissonance as they consider triggering ending crisis leadership activities, divides stakeholders (to the extent that this is ever possible) into those who are:

- permanently negatively affected
- (temporarily) positively affected, or
- temporarily negatively affected.

This allows us to understand in greater detail the dissonance that the crisis leader is likely to experience because, while the bias from the leader personally and that of the organization is typically towards (prematurely) ending crisis leadership, the story outside the organization is more complex.

Let's begin with those who are *temporarily negatively affected* or, in other words, those stakeholders who are suffering from what might be referred to as the 'ripple effect' of the crisis.

These include shareholders who were happy with the returns they were seeing before the crisis began; suppliers for whom the crisis has reduced income from an important customer; and families of those staff who have led the response. The clarion call from each of those stakeholders is for the crisis to end symbolically and in real terms. They wish the resources to be directed as they were before the crisis.

The message from these stakeholders is significant. Not necessarily because it is the voice which generates the most media coverage, nor because it is the most distinctive voice. It is significant because it appeals to the (majority of) crisis leaders and fuels their desire to return to the status quo as quickly as possible.

However, the stakeholders who fall into the *(temporarily) positively affected* and *permanently negatively affected* are also incredibly powerful. They are often united by a common, symbiotic mission to elongate the crisis. However, while their goal is the same it finds its motivation in different places.

In every crisis, there are those stakeholders for whom the situation represents an opportunity to further their own personal or organizational goals. These are the stakeholders who are positively impacted by the crisis, either temporarily or, if the situation is significant enough and/or they are nimble enough to benefit from it, permanently. These can include competitors, non-governmental organizations (NGOs) for whom the crisis is relevant in forwarding their cause, politicians for whom the situation offers a convenient campaigning platform and the media. It also includes, of course, litigation lawyers.

What unites these stakeholders is clearly an organizational gain and, perhaps with the exception of the NGOs and politicians, a commercial gain. Put simply, the longer it continues the better.

And this represents a huge challenge for the crisis leader at the apex of the dissonance. While they (and their organization) may be operating under a deep-rooted desire to return to life as they knew it, most in my experience want to recompense and look after those who have been permanently negatively affected. Yet they have to respond to claims for damages and attacks which often go well beyond what they would consider to be reasonable and proportionate.

It is here, of course, that huge judgement is required. What is reasonable and proportionate? The court of law offers some guidance, but it is often out of sync with the court of public opinion. The crisis leader, in moving towards ending crisis leadership, must help manage this very fine balance.

There are times, of course, when those who are seeking to benefit from the misfortune of others overplay their hand.

The most obvious examples of this are, of course, the litigation lawyers who seek to dramatically increase the numbers of people who can be presented as permanently negatively affected and seek to assign causation to the most deep-pocketed of organizations involved and escalate the damages paid.

The problem is, of course, that any public rebuke of this typically comes far too late to reduce the dissonance the leader feels as he or she prepares to begin the process of ending crisis leadership. The dissonance has to be managed in the interim.

So how does a crisis leader tackle the process of executing the three tasks of collapsing the mechanisms of response, signalling the end of the crisis, and putting the organization on a robust footing for the future? It's not easy. However, sensible guidance can be given. And, having framed these tasks and the dissonance against which they must be executed, that's what I turn my attention to now.

Executing the three tasks of ending crisis leadership

Although I look at standing down the CMT, *bridging and signalling* and *putting the organization on a firm future footing* individually, they are tasks which are

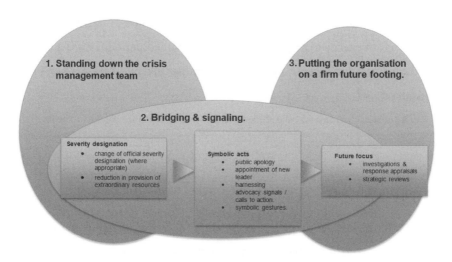

FIGURE 8.3 *The key elements of 'ending' crisis leadership.*

rarely undertaken in the linear, chronological order they are shown in Figure 8.3. Each influences each other the extent of which is determined by the typology of the crisis and the idiosyncrasies of each situation. It's possible, for example, to move from the first activity to the third. Plus, there are a number of bridging and signalling activity, which can vary in nature from the tactical to the strategic, which can be identified and can ease one into another.

However, with these caveats, I hope my generic comments and observations are helpful in deconstructing an aspect of crisis leadership which is as complex as any I have examined so far.

1. Standing down the crisis management team

The decision to stand down the crisis management team and the extraordinary resources brought to bear is a significant moment for any leader. There are prosaic and practical considerations. Returning rooms and equipment to their normal use, for example, is important in reducing the additional mobilized response capacity. And, clearly, it can't be done prematurely. However, it also has an emotional impact on those involved in the response who have dedicated high levels of energy to the response over a sustained period. This is a point I will return to later. As ever, in organizational life there are both hard and soft considerations.

While every situation is different, there are a number of key points that crisis leaders should remember.

Shut down the response gradually and in phases

There are parts of the military which define leadership as being 'what needs to be done'. And there is no better guidance I can give as to the rational considerations which drive the decision to stand down the crisis management team and any relevant additional mechanisms in use (e.g. call centres, loss adjusting teams, reception centres, etc). The leader's responsibility here is to ask what the organization is being called on to provide. Can the situation now be responded to without those extraordinary resources, or with them in diminished form? Has the official severity rating been lowered (a point I return to in detail when I address bridging and signalling activity)? If it can, then consideration clearly needs to be given to collapsing it. Not least as the organizational dissonance will no doubt be pushing for this to happen.

However, it's rare that an organization moves from a full crisis response mechanism to business as usual – a demobilization plan is required. It should happen in stages in order that any remnants of the crisis can be responded to. A variety of work streams will continue for many years at various levels. The peak of the legal response, for example, is likely to come after the peak of the external public scrutiny. Identifying what these peaks are, and ensuring that the appropriate resources are in place and adapting as necessary, is key.

Support staff in the shut down

While it is overwhelmingly true that most of the team will want their life to return to normal, there are some who will find the jolt from operating at high levels of adrenaline for weeks or months on end – with sometimes a clearer and more acute sense of mission than they do in their daily lives – extremely hard to bear. I have on more than one occasion had emotional discussions with CMT members who have felt a severe sense of dislocation when the team is stood down.

The crisis leader should be sensitive to this if the CMT member is to return productively to their previous roles. The provision of counsellors or coaches is not unknown. Taking holiday before recommencing 'business-as-usual' roles is generally recommended.

Ensure documentation is collated and logged

There are fewer heart-stopping moments than when lawyers run through the documents that they want to see as part of 'discovery' during investigations into the crisis, as well, of course, as during criminal or civil proceedings, including any litigation. Sadly, there are few crises which do not include one or all of these elements. Ensuring as the crisis leader that your own notebooks and relevant files, and indeed those of others on the CMT, are filed and easily accessible (even if they are ultimately protected as 'privileged' by the lawyers) is a vital task.

Write things down for yourself

Different but related to that is a step that I always encourage crisis leaders to take, and that is to write down for themselves what happened in broad terms and why they made the decisions they did. Even if this is part of a private journal, it will still be useful.

Few of the decisions a crisis leader makes are straightforward. If they were, there would be no crisis and no need for this book. Plus, most crisis leaders will suffer an agonizing period of *post-decision dissonance*. Put more simply, *did I make the right decision?* Moreover, crisis leaders are very likely to be interrogated on their decisions at some point in the future. Again, this can be years after the event when memories have long since faded.

While the purpose of these (almost) *contemporaneous notes* is primarily pragmatic, only those who have done it will appreciate the cathartic qualities it has. It can help crisis leaders begin their own path towards *closure*.

Keep track of those leaving the organization

Again related is the need to keep track of people who have been a key part of the CMT, but who then go on to leave the organization. Crises can spur people to leave an organization, particularly if they feel the cause of the crisis or the response itself was at odds with their values. For some, crises represent a career wake-up call which prompts them to consider their options or even their broader lifestyle. This all depends on the crisis, the organization and the individual.

However, the sheer length of time that proceedings can take to start, let alone finish, means that it is inevitable that people move on. With them can go vital memories and recollections. The crisis leader should try to find mechanisms to ensure that a professional relationship is maintained. This will nearly always be welcome in the long term.

These tasks seem simple. However, leaders shouldn't underestimate the apparent simplicity of the advice provided. Nor should they be tempted to rush or miss out a phase in a dash to return to their usual lives. They are all being executed in the wake of huge turmoil, the impact of which will go on for years to varying degrees. Ending crisis leadership should be undertaken with the same level of thoughtful diligence as commencing it was.

2. Bridging and signalling

Having looked at the issue of standing down the crisis management team, the crisis leader will be required to lead the organization through a series of what I refer to as 'bridging and signalling' activities. As the moniker suggests, these activities achieve two mutually reinforcing purposes. They:

- signal to stakeholders, internal and external, that the organization is now moving forward. And, in doing so:

- prepare the ground for the organization to put itself on a firm footing for the future;

As shown in figure 8.3, the first set of activities are linked to the standing down of the crisis management team; the second are (usually) symbolic in nature (and often require exquisite judgement in execution), and the third are future-focused.

Not all the activities will be relevant to all crises. Also, the execution of each will be highly crisis-specific. However, they represent a menu of options that can be considered by the crisis leader as he or she seeks to move the crisis into new territory. They demand some investigation.

Severity designation

The business of standing down the crisis management team and with it undertaking the activities I have just explored might be a very internal affair. However, that isn't to say that it isn't prompted by a very external signal.

The most obvious example of this is the change of an official severity designation. Whether it be the lowering of a weather warning, threat of terrorism or indication of disruption, an official body concludes that a certain phase is over.

Making this change can never be done lightly. Such an announcement from an official body is designed to lead to a change in behaviour and/or potentially reduce the provision of and demand for extraordinary resources (from a potentially vast range of organizations which have put themselves on a crisis footing).

The reduction in a weather warning, for example, will lead to members of the public starting to go about their daily lives, businesses to reopen and may trigger the standing down of civil defence contingencies. Such decisions are not made lightly. Typically a range of indicators are used – some hard, but many soft – and these may well include lobbying activity from organizations who have been negatively affected.

Once this announcement has been made, it's hard to reinvoke and achieve the same level of desired behavioural compliance. We are hardwired to look out for examples of official bodies crying wolf. No experienced organization would make such an announcement without significant consideration.

For many organizations, though, the presence of such an external third party and an official indicator is far from unhelpful. It can look to the official body and take guidance.

More difficult is for the organization left to its own devices which is required to announce it is standing down some of the support it has provided in response to a crisis.

Even if the decision to announce such resources are standing down is apparently clear cut due to fall in demand for them, it must be done cautiously and sensitively. Lots of notice is needed and a phased approach nearly always recommended. Stakeholders who were permenantly negatively affected may have a genuine concern that initial support is being withdrawn prematurely. Stakeholders who are temporarily positively affected, for example may be vocal in declaring the organisation reckless or uncaring. As in all aspects of crisis leadership, a keep sense of judgement is needed. The crisis leader must expect some criticism.

Symbolic acts

It's time to draw a line under this and move on – I have lost count of how many times I have heard this statement from exasperated crisis leaders. And I have lost count of how many times I have read this as a sound bite from negatively affected stakeholders commenting in the press about what the impacted organization should do.

It is, of course, an entirely understandable sentiment. Exhausted by the dissonance and increasingly furious at the perceived lack of recognition of the vast efforts that have been dedicated to remediate the problem, it is a natural desire to cry 'leave us alone'.

However, the premature declaration of a desire to have the crisis considered 'over' can unpick months of hard work and self-discipline particularly if the crisis leader who makes the appeal has been convicted by the court of public opinion as the guilty party.

That isn't to say that there aren't statements that can be made or symbolic acts that can't be undertaken which do draw a line under a certain period of a crisis, or at the very least signal that it is moving to a new phase. There are many, in fact. These include

- **A public apology.** The human desire to hear the word 'sorry' runs deep. Hearing a crisis leader apologize can, at times, be enough to propel the organization into a new phase of the crisis.

- **A change of leadership.** There are fewer more impactful signals that the organization is changing direction as a change of leadership. The crisis response can, of course, begin with a change of leadership, typically when the leader is, rightly or wrong, associated with the cause of the crisis. This can come right at the outset of the crisis. Or it can come after the peak of intensity has died down. Dozens of examples of both exist.

- **Getting someone else to do it.** It may be possible to persuade an independent body which has the legitimate moral authority to urge the world to *move on*. Governments might do this on behalf of national champions. Trade bodies which represent an industry are another possible contender.

- **Symbolic gestures.** An organization might decide to divest an asset, leave a country or cease to provide a service. This might be (positioned as being) part of a 'strategic review' (which I touch on later). However, it is actually to distance itself from a part of the organization that has become toxic. Like a tumour, it is simply removed.

It is here that the first signs of genuine opportunity start to reveal themselves. The crisis may provide the platform the organization has long been searching for, or the impetus it needs, to rid itself of a part of the organisation that it no longer wanted anyway.

Whether the crisis leader decides to execute any or all of the activities depends, of course, on the situation itself.

Other than to say that each of the above tasks must be undertaken with an abundance of caution and considerable counsel, it is impossible to give even generic advice on the execution of any of these tasks. Each remains indelibly locked into the idiosyncrasies of the crisis itself and has to be actioned following a rational assessment of the impact they may have. In undertaking one or any of them, what is the crisis leadership trying to achieve?

These are tough decisions for the crisis leadership to make often against a (sometimes quite rightly) febrile backdrop. Any decision they make now may, self evidently, have long-lasting impacts on the orgainsation. That is why they are so closely linked to the final set of bridging and signalling activities.

Future focus

Having (hopefully) drawn a line under the acute phase of the crisis, the leader must now signal that the organization will undertake a thorough review of not just what happened (and why) but also how the organization responded.

I have encountered no organization (of any scale) which has been through a crisis and could mount a legitimate argument as to why it shouldn't conduct such a review. There is simply no legal or moral justification for not doing so. Many questions relating to the methodology of the review and its scope, will need to be answered. However, that such a review should be undertaken should never be questioned.

The second and more wide-ranging tool is to perhaps signal a wide-ranging *strategic review* of the organization and what it does and how it does it. This is more intuitively future-focused, and the scale and depth of the review depends entirely on how existential a threat to the organization the crisis has been. It is also, of course, typically associated with a change in leadership.

In signalling the intent to do one or both of these activities, the crisis leader is once again securing those two vital commodities that the organization needs – *time* and *space*. Having dealt with the initial impact of the crisis, the organization now needs time and space to consider how it moves forward, and time to execute any changes that it may deem necessary or desirable.

However, signalling the intention to undertake either activity is one thing; doing it effectively and then acting upon it is quite another. And it is to that that I now turn as I close the concept of ending crisis leadership by moving the organization onto a robust footing for the future.

3. Putting the organization on a firm future footing

Crises can leave organizations devastated. Drained of energy and beaten up by their stakeholders, they can be hulks of what they once were. The issue facing the crisis leader is, of course, what do we do now?

Stripped back and laid bare, a spectrum of choices are open to the leader, ranging from the (simple) *restoration of the status quo*; to an aspiration to be

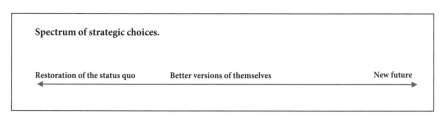

FIGURE 8.4 *The crisis leader's spectrum of strategic choices.*

better versions of themselves; or, at the extreme end, leaders can attempt to create a *new future* for their organization.

The answer as to which represents the most optimal solution for the leader depends, of course, entirely on the crisis, the leader, the organization and the world in which it operates. However, it is possible to make some broad generic comments.

This requires us to look in a bit more detail at executing an investigation and response review and a strategic appraisal, as opposed to just signalling an intent to do so. To start with, I will look at conducting them in the context of the spectrum which runs from the restoration of the status quo to being better versions of themselves.

The restoration of the status quo versus being better versions of themselves

Christophe Roux-Dufort is a Canadian academic who has invested considerable effort in trying to understand why organizations often don't want to learn from crises. Writing in 2002, he noted that:

> Organizations address crises as if they were too exceptional to justify the learning process. The organization's priority is to come back and maintain the status quo as soon as possible rather than explore the extent to which the crisis is a privileged moment during which to understand things differently.[4]

It is my view that no crisis leader should, quite frankly, ever be satisfied with returning to the status quo. It is, at best, cognitively lazy and, at worst, dangerous. Armed with an investigation into what happened and a review as to how the organization responded, they must at least aspire to ensure that the organization executes its tasks more robustly in future. A crisis always brings change.

There are, of course, those leaders who seek to claim that the investigation and subsequent response yielded no lessons. To this my answer is threefold:

- **The organization probably hasn't experienced a real crisis.** The organization has not been under the sort of existential threat that a true crisis brings. Thus, the sorts of changes a crisis nearly always prompts are clearly found to be unnecessary.

- **The investigation and response review weren't fit for purpose.** Investigations and reviews don't happen without effort. Responsible bodies with the right expertise and without conflict of interest (sometimes with figurehead leaders) must be appointed; strict terms of reference are to be defined, and resources, financial and otherwise committed. But as the amplification factors recede, so does the will to instruct an investigation and review properly.

- **The impetus for implementing the lessons is being suppressed.** Even if the report has been a worthwhile endeavour, forces are at work in the individual and in the organization to stop the lessons being implemented.

This third point is not to be dismissed lightly. In my experience, one of the most potent forces in seeking to stop lessons being implemented, or the results of the findings being shared around the organization, are the legal implications. In-house lawyers and external counsel become nervous of disclosure requirements and place the organization on lock down. I am sympathetic to this. The lawyers' role in guiding the organization to act in a way that doesn't endanger it from the pursuit of civil claims (which will go on for years) is understandable. But, taken to its extremes, it is wrong-headed.

And, it is wrong-headed for two reasons. First, if an organization doesn't make changes – and the crisis befalls it again – the situation has, clearly, magnified still further. It is better to have made necessary changes and then explain them, than be found wanting again in future.

Second, to simply seek to restore the status quo is to miss out on the opportunity that a crisis brings. It is here that this notion of crisis bringing opportunity starts to gather a real momentum. I counselled against seeking opportunity during the containment phases I have addressed in Chapter 3. But now it is a genuine consideration.

As Taleb writes in his 2012 book *Antifragile: Things That Gain From Disorder*: Bad events contain useful information; long periods of stability allow risks to accumulate and spring up. Therefore, organizations should recognize that crises give way for improvement, with the gains outweighing the losses.[5]

The plain fact of the matter is that crisis leaders must rally against any softer forces, however powerful they may be, which advocate for a swift return to the status quo.

They should not rest until the learning from the investigation and review is in the process of being implemented and communicated and they are, at the very minimum, becoming *better versions of themselves*. Thus, we will turn our attention briefly to the other end of the spectrum – from better versions to new futures.

Restoring the status quo to defining a 'new future'

History serves up a mixed bag of organizations which, typically after performance crises (sometimes prompted by periods of disruption), have almost entirely reinvented themselves. They have developed missions which are entirely different to the one they had before the crisis

However, the reality is that most organizations which use the learning from the cause of the crisis and the response, combined with a strategic review (that has enough rigour to satisfy Admiral Stockdale), end up being better versions of themselves. And that's no bad thing.

Nor, however, is to underestimate three key points.

First, the transformative impact that this can have on the organization. The implementation of a new of way of approaching an engineering task, or monitoring safety procedures or raising funds seem so simple to write down but they can have a transformative effect on an organization changing the way it and possibly even its industry peers have done something for generations.

It may therefore *feel* to those who works for the orgainsation that it has developed a new future. But its purpose has actually stayed broadly the same.

Second, it therefore means not underestimating the sheer time and space that are required to achieve this better version of themselves. Its seemingly innocuous intent belies the need for vast amounts of work.

The next time you stumble across an article, online or offline, about crisis which probably isn't that long disappeared from the front page or the 'most read' sections, have a look for the timescales the crisis leader has set for transforming his or her organization. They will, of course, need to talk of 'immediate steps' and indeed enact them. However, the effective crisis leader, particularly those seeking to bring 'better change' will almost certainly ask for months if not years to make the changes that they want to make. Whether it's an entire overhaul of its strategy, a complete review of its product portfolio or complete change of its compliance standards, time and space is necessary. The effective crisis leader will not seek to overpromise what can be delivered in the sorts of tiny timescales for which the counterfactuals will be clamouring.

This brings to my third and final point which is to make a few remarks on the complexity that arises out of the subjectivity inherent in the word 'better' when we talk of organisations becoming better versions of themselves.

What is 'better'?

Naturally, all those who are involved in a crisis are united in their desire to ensure that it doesn't happen again and, in doing so, ensure that the organization involved is indeed a 'better version of itself'.

However, though the vast majority of the stakeholders share this same desired outcome, they will not necessarily agree with the crisis leader on the steps he or she believes are necessary to achieve it. On the contrary.

As the crisis leader implements the changes he or she believes are required to make their organizations 'better versions of themselves', criticism should be expected. This will be centred on the fact that for some stakeholders:

- **The changes 'don't go far enough'.** The motivations that drive stakeholders to complain that the proposed changes do not go *deep enough, wide enough* or *long enough* will, of course, differ. At one end of the spectrum will lie those stakeholders who might simply have a different assessment of the cause of the crisis and therefore the steps that need to be taken to stop it from happening again. At the other lie those stakeholders for whom, for whatever reason, the very existence of the organization that suffered the crisis was abhorrent because it was at odds with their values. Absent shutting down the organization in its entirety, they will never approve of the steps taken as long as the organization continues to exist. These stakeholders will never be *satisfied*. And, nor should they be. This is a (part of) the court of public opinion keeping organizations on their toes in its role as regulator without portfolio, as I explored in chapter six.

- **The changes will lead to 'trade-off's some find unacceptable.** Naturally, there are some changes that a crisis leader may wish to make (or may be ordered to make) that have no 'cost' attached, be that financial or otherwise. However, these are few and far between. Most of the changes will lead to a trade-off. Prices may rise and therefore either customers have to pay more or profitability and thus dividends and share prices may fall. A service or product may cease to exist or become less available. A presence in a country or regional location may be withdrawn. Undertaking a task may become more complex or 'burdened with bureaucracy'. A policy or 'position' may be abandoned. These are the often unwelcome side-effects of the steps taken to ensure that the chances of the crisis reoccurring are minimized. Individual members of the court of public opinion may want steps to be taken that minimize the chances of the crisis reoccurring but only those steps which don't affect them personally. As memories of the crisis and its impact recede some will even begin to ask 'What's wrong with the way it used to be done?'

The volume and voracity of the voices from either of these groups depends on many factors including but not limited to how deeply the impact of the original crisis was felt through to how organized the dissatisfied communities of stakeholders are in getting their views heard.

What is clear though is that in putting their organization on a firm future footing, crisis leaders, in addition to buying time and space for the proposed changes to be made effectively, must also *manage expectations*. It will be necessary to acknowledge the fact that the changes coming may be *painful* for some, or *difficult* for others. To promise to please everyone while reducing the chances the crisis may emerge again in the future is a road to nowhere.

So, the concept of being 'better' is far from straightforward. What is 'better' for one set of stakeholders is far from being 'better' for another.

However, there is no need for pessimism as:

1. **managing what I have outlined is a description of what leaders do every day.** To decide how to allocate scarce resources (be they *time, money, energy, focus* or anything else) and, in doing so, decide where *not* to allocate those resources and thus face criticism for their decision is a demand placed on leaders constantly. Not just in a crisis, but every day of the week. Leaders are, or should be, used to it.

2 **the amplification factors will be dimming.** As I have said throughout this book, executing crisis leadership does not require different competencies. Rather it is about exhibiting the *same competencies under different circumstances*. By the time leaders have reached the point of putting the organization on a firm future footing, the extreme amplification factors will have diminished. This will come through the

naturally limited attention span of the media and other stakeholders. But, this will, hopefully, have been aided by the effective execution of some of the bridging and signalling activities I explored earlier in this chapter. And, so, the circumstances that are unfamiliar to the crisis leader gradually give way to the circumstances that he or she knows all too well therefore making the tasks still difficult and uncomfortable but undoubtedly more straightforward to tackle.

There will, naturally, be peaks and troughs of negative external scrutiny as the crisis leader makes missteps along the way as well as other painful moments, perhaps as the legal proceedings which will grumble on reach a particular milestone. However, slowly but surely the organization will return to normal. It may be a *new normal* as the changes implemented begin to become part of the organization's culture. But, as the months and years pass by the crisis will, and should, if the crisis leader has ended crisis leadership effectively, be remembered and talked about positively as something which contributed to making the organization stronger, safer, more robust and therefore, on the whole, *better*.

Conclusion

At the beginning of this chapter I asked you to find a news story in today's media which relates to a crisis which has long since drifted from your consciousness. You may now wish to revisit that story and ask yourself what stage of the journey in 'ending crisis leadership' the crisis leader has reached. And, indeed how much further you think he or she may still need go.

However, I propose that you now look forward rather than back.

The next time an organizational crisis emerges, as it surely will, I strongly urge you to push yourself to maintain interest in what the crisis leader is doing to respond, even when media coverage of it has fallen from the front pages. See if you can identify how and when the crisis response mechanisms were stood down; what bridging and signalling activities the crisis leader executes and how the crisis leader attempts to put the organization on a firm future footing (and deals with the inevitable criticism of the path that is chosen).

The most effective way of learning from the comments made in this chapter – and indeed the whole book – is, of course, to apply them to real-life crises as they emerge. Not just when they lead the day's news during the period of acute crisis but throughout the organization's long period of recovery.

As to what else can be done to help aid the development of future crisis leaders, that is what I turn my attention to now in the final chapter of this book as I explore how to prepare crisis leaders.

HOW CAN CRISIS LEADERSHIP
BE ENDED EFFECTIVELY?

Lessons from the field of public health:
An interview with Dr Keiji Fukuda

There are few people in the world who have executed as much *crisis leadership* as Dr Keiji Fukuda. Dr Fukuda began his career practising medicine on the US West Coast in San Francisco Bay. However, his true calling was in public health. This was a call he answered by joining America's renowned Centre for Disease Control (CDC), where he began to build an unrivalled global expertise in pandemics. While there, he led the CDC's field teams in working with the Hong Kong Department of Health in investigating the first emergence of avian influenza H5N1 in Hong Kong in 1997 and in working as part of World Health Organization (WHO's) efforts to address SARS in Beijing, Shanghai and Hong Kong. In 2005, he joined the WHO, where he has had prominent leadership roles as the WHO responded to the 2009 H1N1 bird flu pandemic and outbreaks of Ebola in 2013 and the emergence of the Middle East respiratory virus in 2012. He is now the organization's Special Representative for Antimicrobial Resistance, undoubtedly one of the most formidable and complex global infectious disease challenges humankind currently faces.

I sat down on a late spring morning with Dr Fukuda at the WHO's headquarters in Geneva to ask him what lessons he had learnt about *ending crisis leadership*.

We begin our discussion in very broad terms, discussing the difference between an *emergency* and a *crisis*. Dr Fukuda recalls his early career as a medical doctor, noting that, for him, an *emergency* is something that requires immediate action and the desired outcome relatively straight forward.

If there is a patient who requires immediate intervention, the objective is clear, he says. It is to save his life. The response for a public health body to a *crisis* is, of course, also to save lives. But, the complexity surrounding how the crisis arose and what can be achieved in response to it, is far more nuanced and uncertain and requires deep consideration, he counsels.

It is in these early exchanges, against the backdrop of the watery Genevan sun with the baby blue of the UN flag fluttering gently in the clean Swiss breeze, that it becomes clear that Dr Fukuda possesses not only the sort of deep intellect one would expect an official at such an august body as the WHO to have, he also has a deep sense of humanity. It is clear that working in public health is, for Dr Fukuda, not a job, it's a vocation.

He notes that his vocation is not an easy one. He touches briefly on the requirement for crisis leaders in public health to be constantly mindful of avoiding accusations of *crying wolf* while also executing its role, which is to work with governments and other partners and to keep them alert and attentive enough to be prepared and ready to combat disease. This balance is one of the biggest challenges that bodies such as the WHO and its crisis leaders must tackle throughout the lifecycle of a threat to the public.

If he feels any frustration at this, then he shows no sign of it. He simply notes that, as a general rule, the WHO adopts a *more information and knowledge is better* approach in tackling crises.

I press Dr Fukuda therefore on what steps are taken by crisis leaders to assess what point of the *lifecycle* a crisis has reached and if indeed the crisis might be *over*.

Before going into detail, he cautions that while a specific outbreak may have passed its peak as a public media event, the wider phenomenon is rarely *over*. The end of a pandemic, for example, does not mean the end of infections or disease or uncertainty. It is for this reason that it is incredibly rare for the WHO to declare something *over*.

Nevertheless, Dr Fukuda concedes that declaring a crisis over, or a threat past its peak and the *ceremony* in doing so, is a watershed moment which:

1   restores a sense of normalcy and relieves potential anxiety among those facing the threat.

2   triggers a change and typically a reduction in the attention and resources given to combatting the threat by all those involved (e.g. governments, health ministries, public bodies and members of the public).

3   prompts a process of learning to begin. Every crisis, says Dr Fukuda, gifts those involved an opportunity learn so they can improve their response in time for the inevitable return of the threat. And, this opportunity must always be taken.

As Dr Fukuda outlines these points, it is abundantly clear why public health officials place such enormous caution in making any form of *declaration*. There is symbolism in such a declaration which helps reduce the inevitable anxiety a crisis brings. However, declarations cause *things to happen* and changes in behaviour across entire communities and even across the entire world. Changes which, if prompted too early, could usher in the premature cessation of actions needed to truly end the threat.

So, how do Dr Fukuda and his colleagues approach getting that timing right? The answer is cautiously and by reviewing every available piece of information to them. And this means examining:

- **Hard intelligence**: this is the raw data and empirical evidence that relates to the threat. Not only must they study the data, but they must also consider the validity of it. For example, is the surveillance in place in the affected countries robust enough to provide believable numbers?

- **Soft intelligence**: these are the media discussions, the volume of questions received behind the scenes by public health bodies and online activity. Dr Fukuda explains that in a globally connected world, the anxiety, speculation and chatter generated by a major health crisis is every bit a part of the crisis as the disease itself. This noise must therefore be closely monitored to judge when levels of anxiety are decreasing.

It is part of our discussion around the use of these different data sources that we touched on the behaviours crisis leaders need to demonstrate to be *effective* crisis leaders.

Listening and communicating are key, says Dr Fukuda, echoing the other crisis leaders I had interviewed. However, he advocates also bringing what he refers to as a sort of *stillness* to the role. For those making decisions in a crisis, he believes, creating emotional and intellectual space or calmness is key to help manage the enormous distractions and constant presentations of *counterfactuals* that a crisis leader has to withstand. These are, he says, particularly acute when analysing what point of its lifecycle the crisis has reached. Behind every counterfactual lurks a possible *agenda*. The crisis leader must see through these agendas and focus on the threat posed to men, woman and children.

Does this sort of analysis lead to a perfect and conclusive answer allowing public health officials the peace of mind to confidently declare a threat either over or, more likely, reduced? No, of course not. Its terrifically hard and requires experience to be used and judgement to be exercised in a situation in which getting it wrong can have profound and grave consequences. But, as Dr Fukuda notes, if it was easy, it wouldn't be a crisis.

Dr Fukuda is an earnest man. To shoulder the responsibilities he has, he would need to be. But, he is warm, amusing and generous with it. And, I observed, during my time with him, ultimately an *optimistic* man. Not one blind to the sheer scale of the crises he has already faced and those that still lie ahead of him. But one sure of the difference that can be made to peoples' lives if the public health crises that emerge are responded to in a diligent but efficacious fashion. In short, Dr Fukuda has the optimal mind-set that any leader, in any walk of life, should have to execute effective crisis leadership. From the outset of the crisis. To its end.

PART THREE

INTRODUCTION

I used part two of this book to investigate both what competencies are required for effective crisis leadership and what behaviours need to be displayed by effective crisis leaders when attending to these tasks. My intention was to take crisis leaders through the lifecycle of a crisis.

In part three, I investigate how, apart from reading this book, crisis leaders can and should ensure that they are in the best possible position to execute effective crisis leadership. And what the influencers who surround leaders can do to play their part in preparing crisis leaders.

9

Preparing crisis leaders

Around fifteen years ago, I took part in a crisis simulation exercise. Although it was still very early as I made my way to the client's office, it was obviously going to be one of those blisteringly hot London days. They may be rare, but they do happen. And, there was a large part of me that would have preferred to enjoy a cup of coffee in the sun by the river than take part in an exercise that would put members of the senior leadership of a major corporation through its paces against a very testing scenario.

However, I am glad I didn't succumb because this was the day when my deep interest in crisis leadership began.

My role on the day was to observe how the leader of the most senior team, the CMT, responded to the scenario. Without putting too fine a point on it, the gentleman I was observing was, quite simply, inspiring.

He spent time understanding the scenario put in front of him; he could articulate very clearly the role he thought his organization should be taking in the response; he knew what he wanted his organization to achieve (and knew what it couldn't); and he listened carefully to the (frequently) opposing views of the team around him before gently but firmly allocating actions. Then, between formal meetings of his team, he took himself on what can only be described as the cognitive equivalent of heavy work out, along with selected members of his CMT. *How could the situation get worse? What would prompt it do so? And, if so, would we have the capacity to respond to that?* And so it went on.

Wow, I thought. If only I could teach leaders to do what he did and how he did it.

These were fledgling views. I have, in the intervening years, had the great privilege of advising and working alongside many crisis leaders during countless exercises, but, perhaps more importantly, during many live crises. And I have learnt something from each of them. I now know that the gentleman I observed a decade and half ago would have benefited from seeing other crisis leaders, and they from observing him.

My intention therefore in this book has been to fuse together the very best of all of them in one place in order that these crisis leaders can, to an extent at least, see each other and learn from one another.

However, leaders are influenced by many people and many things. And, I believe that many of the sources of influence – including the organizations they work for, trade bodies and business schools – could do more to help leaders prepare for the challenges of crisis leadership. I use this final chapter to outline what I believe they should be doing to prepare crisis leaders.

The journey so far

In other chapters of this book, I have tried to 'frame' the content. Rather than try to simply tell leaders how, I believe, they should tackle a certain task in crisis conditions, I have outlined (and to some extent sympathized with) why I believe the task is hard. The challenges of preparing crisis leaders must also be framed correctly if they are to be fully appreciated. I am going to do that in this chapter by summarizing, briefly, what has been covered so far.

This book has been structured around a series of competencies (*knowledge, skills and abilities*) that I believe crisis leaders need to be able to demonstrate during a crisis.

Some readers may find it depressing or confusing that I have found it necessary to spell out that effective crisis leaders need to accurately diagnose the problem, remind their team of their mission, set objectives and then allocate tasks accordingly etc.

To this point, I would make three comments:

- **First, far from depressing, it's good news.** Surely it's a positive observation that there isn't a whole new set of leadership competencies that need to be learnt to be an effective crisis leader. While it's different, it's also the same. This leads to economies of learning and development.

- **Second, those readers who find it confusing are those who underestimate the challenge of these basic leadership skills in peacetime (and have not experienced the disorientating effects of a crisis).** When working with clients I often make the observation that the production of a simple set of (strategic) objectives, for example, during peacetime can, on the face of it, seem an anticlimax when they are presented after months of work and millions of dollars invested in strategy consultants. Those few words surely can't be what all the fuss was about? But settling on objectives is very hard. It is the tip of the iceberg of consideration and consultation. Settling on objectives at hyperspeed against the disorientating amplification factors of a crisis makes a hard task much harder.

- **Third, that is why I have expended exponentially more effort on *how* rather than *what*.** The vast majority of the words in most chapters are given not to the what but the how. They are dedicated to describing some of the high-performing behaviours I have seen effective crisis leaders display when executing the competencies I have identified as being important. That is not to say that they are the right behaviours. They are merely those I have seen work most effectively when leaders are battling the headwinds of the amplification factors.

This last point requires to me to make an observation about what I have tried strenuously to avoid doing throughout this book, and that is to discuss personality traits.

That is not because they are not relevant. On the contrary. Behaviours (the *how*) that leaders adopt in their execution of crisis leadership are surface-level actions which are observable to followers. And they are clearly linked to the underlying personality construct of the leader themselves. Thus, personality traits are highly relevant and need to be considered by the leader, as they indeed provide a challenge to the leader when attempting to display the behaviours I have outlined earlier.

However, some perspective is required. Personality traits are not immovable barriers. They do not set us on predetermined a course to exhibit the same behaviours, irrespective of whether we want to display them. There is no take it or leave it.

Every day, successful leaders are required to have high levels of emotional intelligence, which doesn't mean that they smooth over their personality traits entirely. Rather, it means that they marshal themselves to be the best they can be and thus display the behaviours they know are effective.

The danger in a crisis is that the amygdala takes over and they are less able to marshal the behaviours they wish to demonstrate and those outlined in this book that I counsel are most effective.

To counter this, leaders need to ensure that they are in the best possible position, should it be required, to demonstrate effective crisis leadership behaviours and, of course, to undertake the identified competencies. But what can leaders do to prepare themselves?

Effective crisis leaders should prepare themselves

To an extent, leaning on existing executive development initiatives which may already exist in thier own organisations is a helpful first start. However, I think there is more that leaders themselves should be doing. They should be engaging in, learning from and actively observing aspects of themselves, their organizations, their immediate operating environment and indeed the wider world around them.

In very specific terms, leaders should:

- **Examine their own behaviours in situations akin to crisis circumstances.** While crises are unique in that they combine the sum of all (or at least most) of the amplifications factors I have introduced in Chapter 2, other situations can be 'stressful'. This may be because they contain one or two of the amplifications factors. Leaders are exposed to them separately and constantly. They should examine situations that they are experiencing as stressful, consider which of the amplifications factors might be at play, consider how their behaviours change, and think about what coping mechanisms they might deploy to ensure that their behaviours remain effective. The braver ones might ask for their followers' feedback on how their behaviour changes in such circumstances (if it does) and what impact such a change has on them.

- **They should actively engage in their organization's crisis preparedness activities.** One of the easiest ways for leaders to assess how they respond to amplification factors is to take part in crisis simulation exercises. That is, after all, what they are there for. They may not be perfect simulations, but I have lost count of the number of crisis leaders who have said to me how similar exercises have felt to the live crises they have experienced. However, crisis leaders need to do more than simply take part in exercises. They need to engage in, read, digest, constructively criticize and help develop the procedures that drive a rapid crisis response. Doing this will relieve the cognitive load in a crisis and allow them to focus less on the procedures and more on the management of their own behaviours and those around them in the event of a live crisis. I have seen too many leaders flounder in the opening hours and days of a crisis, with both the *what* and the *how*, to have any time whatsoever for the dismissive 'I haven't read the procedures, we'd be able to cope' line so often heard from potential crisis leaders when they are asked if they have read the plans in place in their organization. Tellingly, in my experience it is those leaders who have experienced a crisis who typically engage most thoroughly in these preparedness initiatives.

- **They should reach out to stakeholders of all kinds, be they followers, potential collaborators or influencers.** As I have explored in Chapter 3, crises are defined by the fact that many different stakeholders are typically involved in the response. And, as I have also explained, that typically involves conflicts and, frequently, a jostling for position as missions become confused among the responding organizations and the search for an opportunity to exploit the situation for their own ends becomes apparent. The management of this during a crisis is materially easier if the crisis leader knows their opposite number and can call on established relationships with counterparts at those organizations that are likely to join any response. Pragmatism remains key. And this can so often be done through the commitment of the crisis leader to their day-to-day stakeholder relations activities. These are often sent to the bottom of the to-do list, as leaders succumb to internal demands. However, effective crisis leaders look 'out' as much as they look 'in'.

- **Critically and thoughtfully observe other leaders as they respond to crises.** I am often surprised at the superficial observation that leaders make about other leaders who are in the public eye responding to a crisis. Even the sharpest of organizational leaders have, in my experience, a tendency to dismiss the response of other leaders without critical appraisal of the constraints in which they are operating or indeed observant analysis of the tactics and techniques they are deploying, whether that is in the containment phase or indeed in the hunt for organizational time and space to bring crisis leadership to an end. This is such a missed opportunity. Potential crisis leaders should seize any opportunity they can to further their understanding of what does and does not lead to effective crisis leadership. And this interest should extend beyond the period of peak media interest. Leaders should avoid becoming part of the mass, ill-disciplined jury in the court of public opinion. Today's operating environment will continue to provide plenty of examples of crisis leadership, both effective and ineffective.

Other leadership influencers could do more

Inherent in being a leader is a requirement for self-development and a commitment to constantly evaluate and evolve readiness to lead, whatever the requirement. That's why I began with the counsel outlined above.

However, leaders do not lead or *self-develop* in a vacuum. They work within structures; they influence and are influenced by individuals and organizations which operate in all of the layers outlined in Figure 9.1.

However, I believe that many of the organizations which exist in those layers and work to influence leaders could do much more to help prepare leaders for crisis leadership. Specifically, I think that the organizations leaders work for, the trade associations which represent them, the business schools which educate them and the consultants who advise them could all do much more.

There are, of course, other organizations that exist in these *layers* – regulators, for example. However, I cannot recommend that regulators become embroiled too deeply in the notion of preparing crisis leaders. Yes, they need

**Leaders should prepare
themselves by learning from
multiple layers**

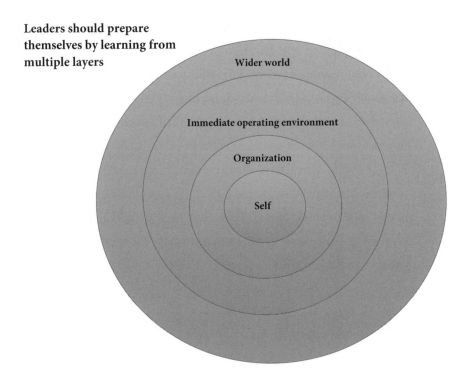

FIGURE 9.1 *The various layers the (potential future) crisis leader must observe.*

to set minimum standards on technical issues that are relevant to the cause of crises. These could range from capital requirements on bank balance sheets through to the sorts of equipment needed to deal with oil spills.

However, to become deeply involved in crisis leadership is to expose themselves to *regulatory capture*. Regulators don't want to do the job of those they regulate. Nor should they have to.

The media also exists in these layers. Wouldn't it be wonderful if the media played its role in helping to prepare crisis leaders (and giving them more latitude to respond in a live crisis) by not presenting grotesquely complex problems, of the sort that leaders have to face during a crisis, as being a choice between 'right' and 'wrong'?

Sadly, that isn't going to happen. While media oversimplification often goes far too far, its bellicose rant keeps leaders sharp and drives them onwards to

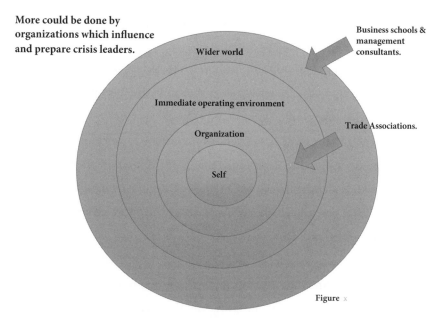

More could be done by organizations which influence and prepare crisis leaders.

Business schools & management consultants.

Wider world

Immediate operating environment

Organization

Self

Trade Associations.

Figure x

FIGURE 9.2 *The improvements that could be made to preparing crisis leaders.*

find resolution. And it helps leaders work hard to avoid finding themselves in a crisis in the first place. A free media is, of course, on the whole, a force for tremendous good.

So I restrict myself to urging change in places where I believe change could and should be made. I start with the organizations for which the crisis leader works.

Organizations need to demonstrate true commitment to crisis management and crisis leadership

I have noted that the first source from which a crisis leader should take inspiration and opportunity to prepare themselves for crisis leadership is the organization itself. They should, for example, take part in crisis simulation exercises. However, to do this effectively, the organization must have a set of a preparedness initiatives in place (e.g. running a programme of crisis simulations) for them to engage with.

This may seem like an odd comment to make. Surely, if there is nothing in place then it is up to the leadership to ensure something is implemented? It's two sides of the same coin.

That's true to an extent. However, it's important to remember the point that was made in Chapter 2, which is that there is a requirement for many different crisis leaders in a crisis. A CMT leader may not be the CEO. In fact, it often isn't. Thus, potential crisis leaders may lack the direct authority to install robust crisis initiatives.

However, such crisis leaders must lobby for crisis preparedness initiatives to be installed if they find their organization's preparedness wanting and they lack the authority to kick-start it themselves. And the organization should listen.

Sadly, as the evidence presented in Chapter 2 suggests, that is not enough. Today's organizations are complex and disparate, with supply chains that snake around the globe, serving customers' needs at ever-increasing speed. They do so in a chaotic and disrupted world which binds its companies, charities and public bodies to a kaleidoscope of complex regulations and shifting expectations. At the risk of hyperbole, the potential for a crisis lurks around many corners.

Much of what I believe organizations should do to ensure that crisis leaders are influenced and supported are covered in Chapter 2. However, in summary, it is my strong belief that organizations need to:

- **Accept that crises can and do happen, and their own organization's future is not assured.** Anything could happen. Optimism bias is necessarily evident from the bottom of the organization right to the top. This needs to be rebalanced. Senior leadership needs to set the right tone. It should stop viewing risk as an annoying existential concept that needs brief acknowledgement in the context of possible threats to the organization achieving its strategic goals. Rather, strategic risk, that is potential threats to the viability of the organization, should not be assessed in isolation from the opportunities facing the organization. Consideration should be given to what steps can be taken to assure the future of the organization as a baseline strategic goal. Opportunities should be considered only once we know that the organization is protected enough to pursue them.

- **Integrate risk management more closely with crisis management.** The current lack of true regard for risk management at a strategic level feeds, of course, its execution at lower levels. Risk management is too frequently relegated to boxes being ticked in a spreadsheet, reviewed by almost no one, the outcome of which is less about mitigating the risk but more about giving an executive the ability to say to the Board that risk is being 'managed'. Too often it's little more than crossing our fingers behind our back. But not that much more.

  There are reasons for optimism. The traditional ways of mapping risk at these more operational levels – which meant siloing risks along country, divisional or service lines – are making way for assessment of cross-organizational threats such as cyber or governance failures. Risk is then more effectively viewed horizontally. At the same time, greater consideration is being given to how to integrate related 'risk' disciplines, such as disaster recovery and business continuity management. However, there is still work to do vertically. In many organizations, the top of the process has been left off. What do I mean by that?

  Crisis management ought, of course, to be the final protective measure that swings into action when all risk mitigation measures have failed. Particularly for those crises that sit in the performance or policy categories, there is a fluidity between a crisis' origins and its move through the lifecycle should risk mitigation measures fail.

Yet crisis management remains a nomadic function, the ownership of which roams around the organization via the path of least resistance, frequently entirely divorced from the risk management function. This means crisis leaders are often required to take control of situations that have been developing for many months. A more fluid approach would leave the crisis leader benefitting from greater knowledge of a developing situation, thus being more effective should the risk mature into a crisis. This needs to change, and *risk management* needs to be sealed in with *crisis management*.

Crisis management structures need to be opened up to a broader range of crises. Possibly because of its orphan status, crisis management structures are behind risk management in accepting that crisis typologies no longer obediently sit in neat boxes. And yet crisis management is still too narrowly focused on responding to the most historically obvious of risks faced by an organization.

If you asked an executive of an oil company to consider how he or she would respond to a *cyber crisis*, they would almost certainly not reference the organization's crisis management team. Intuitively, they would consider the crisis management team's role to be to respond to oil spills. But what if the company's systems had been breached and its remote, computer-controlled offshore drilling platforms had been hacked, taken control of and oil had been deliberately spilled as a result? Organizations therefore must consider more generic and flexible structures to ensure the crisis leader has what they need in order to respond effectively.

- **Foster a culture which celebrates the characteristics of the very best of high-reliability organizations.** Finally, and perhaps most self-evidently, organizational leaders need to adopt behaviours that are characterstic of those high-reliability organizations I have outlined in Chapter 2. Quite apart from preventing the likelihood of a crisis occurring in the first place, for a crisis leader to be surrounded by followers who are used to operating in an environment that is committed to those notions is to be surrounded by a greatly increased potential for success. Sadly, many organizations are yet to make such a commitment. This is another factor that needs to change. And it needs to do so in both large and complex organizations (which, in my experience, are typically more inclined to do so) but also in smaller ones. This must, of course, be done appropriately. What suits a multibillion dollar, global company won't suit a small charity. However, I find the words 'innovative' and 'entrepreneurial' are often used to describe organizations which are, frankly, just badly run. Potential crisis leaders should lobby for the sort of behaviours that are badly needed and organizations should respond.

Trade associations need to do more to share the learning of crisis leaders

In undertaking their remit of protecting and promoting the industry they represent, trade associations are typically driven by their largest and most influential member (as that's the member which often makes the largest financial contribution). They spend much of their time engaged in understanding and influencing policy and becoming involved in the direct and positive commercial interests of the member organization. However, in all fairness, most also act as a conduit through which members can learn from each other. And this is where their role in preparing crisis leaders emerges.

In the aftermath of a crisis, the trade bodies should not only swing into action to represent the industry (and possibly negotiate with the regulator on its regulatory response), they should also ensure that the stories of the leadership that was involved in the response are heard by (potential) crisis leaders from other member organizations.

The CEO's of the trade bodies should challenge reluctance from the crisis leadership to share their story, they should create spaces in which those stories can be told and encourage other potential crisis leaders to attend and hear them. For those trade bodies which offer qualifications and accreditations, such stories should influence the training and professional education they provide.

Their interest in doing this ought not need spelling out. A failed crisis leader can tarnish a whole industry, the impact of which will be felt in many ways and possibly over many years. Trade bodies' interests and those of their member organizations are thus in lockstep. Or, at least they should be.

Executive educators need to update their PowerPoint slides

Executive educators are, I believe, another community which could do more to help prepare potential crisis leaders.

The influence of business schools is staggering. According to research by the *Financial Times*, nearly a third of the world's largest five hundred companies by market capitalization have a CEO with an MBA.[1] And the qualification frequently tops the charts as the most popular postgraduate programme, aided no doubt by the now dizzying array of types of MBA to choose from.

Given this success and experience, one might be forgiven for thinking that the role of the business school was fairly intuitive. They are surely there to prepare leaders for contemporary leadership challenges?

Yet the business school community is far from beyond contorting itself into convulsions of angst on this metter. In a now infamous *Harvard Business Review* article, in 2005, W. G. Bennis and J. O'Toole launched a broadside on business schools for measuring themselves on the rigour of their academic research rather than their graduates' understanding of business drivers.[2] (W. G. Bennis reflects on the violent response of some business school deans to this in a later article for business news provider, Bloomberg, in which he regales readers with the story of one who tore up and stamped on the offending article, at a welcoming speech.)[3]

In some ways, the debate has developed. Data relating to the performance of business schools, and, more importantly, their graduates, are now sliced and diced by, it would appear, every (professional) magazine and newspaper in the world.

As the Academy of Management notes in a collection of articles, criticism of the business schools continues. And that is for a variety of reasons, including their current failure to help prepare crisis leaders or prepare their students to lead in a crisis.[4]

This has been most effectively articulated by behavioural scientist (and business school faculty member), Dr David De Cremer, writing in the *Financial Times* in 2012. He believes that the 2008 financial crises revealed that the world lacks leaders who can deal with uncertainty.[5] He goes on to concede that business schools may have created a blind spot through the creation of too much positivity bias. Or, in other words, students are led to believe that excellence is the only state they can learn from. This call for reflection echoes my earlier recommendation that leaders need to observe more closely and more intelligently how other leaders in crises are behaving. Business schools should heed his call.

However, it's De Cremer's call for business schools to help leaders understand uncertainty and the nature of it – one of the amplification factors – that I agree with the most. In fact, I would go further. Business schools need to address the issue of crisis leadership and crisis management specifically. Surely the seemingly endless slew of previously unthinkable organizational crises, along with the executive careers they have brought to an end (or at least stalled), is impetus enough?

Yet the evidence that the business world has responded to and begun to meet this need is scant. Of the leading business schools around the world, only Michigan's Ross School of Business passes the test with its MBA Leadership Challenge, an initiative that promises to prepare students to 'lead in a high-pressure, high-stakes environment'. Full marks to Michigan.

Why the other seats of leadership do not do this, I don't know. But to achieve their mission of preparing leaders for the challenges of contemporary organizational life, they surely should.

Crisis management consultants

Last, but not the least, I come to the business of management consultants or, more specifically, crisis management consultants, the discipline in which I have spent my working life. It too could, and indeed should, do more to prepare crisis leaders.

For too long, crisis management consultants have focused on the process of crisis management contingency plan writing, and ignored the needs and fears of the people called upon to lead the organization when such plans are invoked.

This is perhaps not such a surprise. Such plans do need to be written. And, in defence of the industry, they are being written with ever greater sophistication, depth and creativity. Gone are the days when former policemen or military service personnel or public relations advisers would sit isolated from their clients and draft a magnum opus of dry, generic words that would be consigned to lever arch files and would sit like a tomb stone on the shelves of executives who were too busy to notice its existence, let alone read it.

These days, crisis management plans are dynamic initiatives (rather than staid documents), written in collaboration and consultation with (rather than splendid isolation from) a wide variety of representatives from their client organization (rather than delivered to a single department). They are simpler but rich in their flexibility, reflecting their need to encompass a wider variety of potential crises which may need to be responded to, rather than codifying the response to one type of crisis which stays obediently within its matrix. The plans also reflect a collision of resilience disciplines which combine disaster recovery, business continuity management, cyber integrity, security management, environmental sustainability and stakeholder engagement. Today's crisis management consultants have to be intellectually curious and vocationally nimble, while at the same time having a talent for organizational diplomacy.

This has innumerable benefits for the crisis leader. It means the plans that are invoked to support the response are, frankly, much better. But they still address the organizational and not the individual response. Supporting crisis leaders is something consultants continue to shy away from.

I don't know why this should be the case. I have seen valiant efforts to support and prepare crisis leaders. Sadly, though, they have often been from those former police or military men, who try and encourage organizational leaders to do it as they once did it, in the police or in the army. But their clients aren't in the police or the army. They are in companies, or charities, or political parties, or complex multilateral bodies. They have tried to convince them that crises require different leadership. And that's the problem. They don't. They simply need to demonstrate the same leadership … just under different circumstances. And there lies the key to success.

To put it simply, to support crisis leaders crisis management consultants need to:

- **Understand leadership.** Not special leadership. Not different leadership. Just the well-worn yet complex tenets of organizational leadership in today's world. They need to understand its key theories, basic tenets and the lexicon that is used to bring it to life.

- **Provide the platforms that leaders need to practise leadership under the circumstances that a crisis brings**. The crisis simulations – in all the forms they can take, which are so beloved by the consultants and so needed by their clients – must test the leader's ability not do something different but instead to do the same things they do every day, against the amplification factors that only a crisis can bring and which present such seemingly insurmountable challenges to leadership.

As in so many areas of consultancy, the value lies in seeing and pointing out what others either don't see or are unable to raise as a problem (for so many reasons) rather than finding and explaining a complexity that actually doesn't exist.

In conclusion

And that's it. What I have proposed here is not onerous, neither for the potential crisis leader nor for the influencers who exist around the crisis leader.

Not only that, but the steps that I propose the crisis leader takes are beneficial not just in crises. They are help leaders to execute their leadership responsibilities each and every day.

The steps I propose for the organizations and institutions that influence the crisis leader would surely also be to their benefit, by any measure, commercial or otherwise. The notion of a crisis (or, at least being prepared for one) throws up the potential for opportunity.

Will the potential crisis leaders or those who surround them undertake the steps I propose? I don't know. But I hope so. Because if they do, when or if the moment comes for a leader to become a crisis leader, they will have the very best possible chance of bringing themselves (and their organization) through the toughest and most gruelling professional challenge they are likely to face. Ever.

NOTES

Chapter 1

1 Koselleck, R. and Richter, M. (2006), 'Crisis'. *Journal of the History of Ideas*, 67(2), 357–400.

2 Taleb, N. (2007), *The Black Swan: The Impact of the Highly Improbable*, 2nd edn. London: Penguin Books Ltd.

3 James. H. E. and Wooten, L. P. (2005), 'Leadership as (un)usual: How to display competence in times of crisis', *Organizational Dynamics*, 34(2), 141–52.

4 Ulmer, R. R., Sellnow, T. L. and Seeger, M. W. (2007), *Effective Crisis Communication: Moving from Crisis to Opportunity*, 2nd edn. London: SAGE Publications Ltd.

5 British Standards Institution (2014), *BS 11200:2014 Crisis Management – Guidance and Good Practice*. London: BSI.

6 Pearson, C. M. and Clair, J. A. (1998), 'Reframing crisis management'. *Academy of Management Review*, 23(1), 59–76.

7 DuBrin, A. J. (2013), *Handbook of Research on Crisis Leadership in Organizations*. London: Edward Elgar Publishing Ltd.

8 Giles, S. (2016), 'The most important leadership competencies, according to leaders around the world'. *Harvard Business Review.* Available from: https://hbr.org (Accessed 15 June 2016).

9 Feser, C., Mayol, F. and Srinivasan, R. (2015), 'Decoding leadership: What really matters'. *McKinsey Quarterly.* Available from: http://www.mckinsey.com (Accessed 15 June 2016).

Chapter 2

1 British Standards Institution (2014), *BS 11200:2014 Crisis Management – Guidance and Good Practice*. London: BSI.

2 Geithner, T. F. (2015), *Stress Test: Reflections on Financial Crises*. New York: Crown Publishers.

3 Allio, R. J. (2009), 'Leadership – the five big ideas'. *Strategy and Leadership*. 37(2), 4–12.

4 Bennis, W. (1999), 'The leadership advantage'. *Leader to Leader*, 12, 18–23.

5 Tiger, L. (1995), *Optimism: The Biology of Hope*, 2nd edn. New York: Kodansha America Inc.

6 Kahneman, D. (2011), *Thinking Fast and Slow*. London: Penguin Books.

7 *The Economist*. 'The Slumps that Shaped Modern Finance'. Available from: http://www.economist.com (Accessed 2 March 2017)

8 Deloitte. (2016), 'A Crisis of Confidence'. Deloitte Touche Tohmatsu Limited.

9 Jaques, T. (2011), 'Barriers to effective crisis preparedness: CEOs assess the challenges'. *Asia Pacific Public Relations Journal*, 12(2), 1–11.

10 Deal, T. E., and Kennedy, A. A. (1982), *Corporate Cultures: The Rites and Rituals of Corporate Life*. Reading, MA: Addison-Wesley Pub. Co.

11 Schein, E. H. (2004), *Organizational Culture and Leadership*, 3rd edn. San Francisco: Jossey-Bass.

12 Johnson, G., Scholes, K. and Whittington, R. (2008), *Exploring Corporate Strategy*, 8th edn. London: Financial Times Prentice Hall.

13 Deal, T. E., and Kennedy, A. A. (1982), *Corporate Cultures: The Rites and Rituals of Corporate Life*. Reading, MA: Addison-Wesley Pub. Co.

14 Whittingham, R. B. (2004), *The Blame Machine. Why Human Error Causes Accidents*. Oxford: Elsevier.

15 Perrow, C. (1999), *Normal Accidents: Living with High-Risk Technologies*. Princeton, NJ: Princeton University Press.

16 Weick, K. E., Sutcliffe K. M. and Obstfeld, D. (1999), 'Organizing for high reliability: process of collective mindfulness'. In Sutton, R. S. and Staw, B. M. (eds), *Research in Organizational Behavior, Volume 1*. Stanford: Jai Press, pp. 81–123.

17 Weick, K. E. and Sutcliffe, K. M. (2001), *Managing the Unexpected: Assuring High Performance in an Age of Complexity*. San Francisco: Jossey-Bass.

18 IPIECA (2015), 'Tiered preparedness and response'. *IPIECA*. Available from: http://www.ipieca.org (Accessed 2 March 2017).

19 The issue of declaring a situation a 'crisis' or not is relevant here. It is typical of many organizations to have a senior fail safe point in the mechanism at which a senior stakeholder can assess the information provided and mobilize the teams accordingly.

Chapter 3

1   Johnson, G., Scholes, K. and Whittington, R. (2008), *Exploring Corporate Strategy*, 8th edn. London: Financial Times Prentice Hall.

2   Goleman, D. (2011), *Leadership: The Power of Emotional Intelligence: Selected Writings*. Massachusetts: More Than Sound.

3   Goleman, D. (1996), *Emotional Intelligence: Why it can matter more than IQ*. London: Bloomsbury Publishing Plc.

4   National Geographic (2011), 'George W. Bush: The 9/11 Interview'. National Geographic Channel.

5   Cooper, G. E., White, M. D. and Lauber, J. K. (1980), 'Resource Management on the flight deck'. *NASA*.

6   Gawande, A. (2011), *The Checklist Manifesto*. New York: Henry Holt and Company.

7   Lewis, M. (2010), *The Big Short: Inside the Doomsday Machine*. London: Allen Lane.

8   Bennett, N. and Lemoine, J. G. (2014), 'What VUCA Really Means for You'. *Harvard Business Review*. Available from: https://hbr.org (Accessed 02 March 2017).

Chapter 4

1   McChrystal, G. S., Collins, T., Silverman, D. and Fussell, C. (2015), *Team of Teams: New Rules of Engagement for a Complex World*. London: Portfolio Penguin.

2   Jung, C. G. (1963), *Memories, Dreams, Reflections*. New York: Vintage Books.

3   Mitroff, I. and Pauchant, T. C. (1992), *Transforming the Crisis-Prone Organization: Preventing individual, organizational, and environmental tragedies*. California: Jossey-Bass.

4   Adams, J. B., Dust, S. B. and Piccolo, R. F. (2013), 'Approaches to minimize choking under pressure'. In DuBrin, A. J. (eds), *Handbook of Research on Crisis Leadership in Organizations*. Cheltenham: Edward Elgar Publishing Limited, pp. 23–44.

5   Collins, J. and Porras, J. I. (2005), *Built to Last: Successful Habits of Visionary Companies*, 10th ed. London: Random House Business Books.

6   Buchanan, L. and O'Connell, A. (2006), 'A brief history of decision making'. *Harvard Business Review*. Available from: https://hbr.org/2006/01/a-brief-history-of-decision-making (Accessed 5 December 2016).

7   Damasio, A. (2005), *Descartes' Error: Emotion, Reason, and the Human Brain*. London: Penguin.

8 Maslow, A. H. (1943), 'A Theory of Human Motivation'. *Psychological Review,* 50(4), 370–96.

9 Lewis, M. (2012), 'Obama's Way'. *Vanity Fair.* Available from: http://www.vanityfair.com/news/2012/10/michael-lewis-profile-barack-obama (Accessed 30 December 2016).

10 Mintzberg, H. (1987), 'The Strategy Concept II: Another Look at Why Organizations Need Strategies'. *California Management Review* 58 (4), 25–32.

11 Goodman, N. (1947), 'The Problem of Counterfactual Conditionals'. *The Journal of Philosophy* 44(5), 113–28.

12 Zaremba, A. J. (2009), *Crisis Communication: Theory and Practice.* New York: M. E. Sharpe.

13 Festinger, L. (1957), *A Theory of Cognitive Dissonance.* Evanston, IL: Row & Peterson.

14 Earley, J. S. (1979), *The Collected Writings of John Maynard Keynes. Activities 1939-1945: Internal War Finance,* by Donald Moggridge and John Maynard Keynes. Reviewed in *Journal of Economic Literature* 17(2), 539–41.

15 Baumeister, R. F. and Tierney J. (2009), *Willpower: Rediscovering the Greatest Human Strength.* London: Penguin Books.

16 Collins, J. and Porras, J. I. (2005), *Built to Last: Successful Habits of Visionary Companies,* 10th ed. London: Random House Business Books.

17 Rittel, H. W. and Webber, M. M. (1973), 'Dilemmas in a General Theory of Planning'. *Policy Sciences* 4 (2), 155–69.

18 Ackoff, R. L. (1974), *Redesigning the Future: a Systems Approach to Societal Problems.* New York: John Wiley & Sons.

19 Camillus, J. C. (2008), 'Strategy as a Wicked Problem'. *Harvard Business Review.* Available from: www.hbr.org (Accessed 30 November 2016).

20 Grint, K. (2005), 'Problems, problems, problems: The social construction of "leadership"'. *Human Relations* 58 (11), 1467–94.

21 Conklin, J. E. and Weil, W. (1998), 'Wicked Problems: Naming the Pain in Organization'. [Online] Available from: http://www.leanconstruction.dk/media/17537/Wicked_Problems__Naming_the_Pain_in_Organizations_.pdf (Accessed 20 December 2016).

22 Ackoff, R. L. (1979), 'The Future of Operational Research is Past'. *The Journal of the Operational Research Society* 30 (2), 93–104.

23 Hofstadter, D. R. (1986), *Metamagical Themas: Questing for the Essence of Mind and Patter.* New York: Basic Books.

24 Klein, G., Moon, B. and Hoffman, R. R. (2006), 'Making Sense of Sensemaking 1: Alternative Perspectives'. *IEEE Computer Society* 21(4), 70–3.

25 Regester, M., and Larkin, J. (2008), *Risk, Issues and Crisis Management in Public Relations,* 4th ed. London: Kogan Page.

26 Kahneman, D. (2011), *Thinking Fast and Slow*. London: Penguin Books.

27 Mintzberg, H. (1987), 'The Strategy Concept II: Another look at why organizations need strategies'. *California Management Review* 30 (1), 25–32.

28 Thaler, R. H. and Sunstein, C. R. (2009), *Nudge: Improving Decisions about Health, Wealth and Happiness*. London: Penguin Books Ltd.

29 Syed, M. (2015), *Black Box Thinking: The Surprising Truth About Success*. London: John Murray Publishers.

Chapter 5

1 Kozlowski, S. W. K. and Bell, B. S. (2003), 'Work groups and teams in organizations'. In Borman, W. C., Ilgen, D. R. and Klimoski, R. J. (eds), Handbook of psychology (Volume 12): Industrial and organizational psychology. New York: John Wiley & Sons, pp. 333–75.

2 Hackman, R. (1998), 'Why Teams Don't Work'. *Leader to Leader*, 1998 (7), 24–31.

3 Hackman, R. (1998), 'Why Teams Don't Work'. In Tindale, R. S., Heath, L., Edwards, J., Emil, J., Posavac, E. J., Bryant, F. B., Suarez-Balcazar, Y., Henderson-King, E. and Myers, J. (eds), *Theory and Research on Small Groups*. New York: Plenum Press, pp. 245–67.

4 Beckhard, R. (1972), 'Optimizing Team Building Efforts'. *Journal of Contemporary Business*, 1 (3), 23–32.

5 Tichy, N. M. and Cohen, E. (2002), *The Leadership Engine*. New York: Harper Business Essentials.

6 Lencioni, P. (2002), *The Five Dysfunctions of a Team: A Leadership Fable*. San Francisco: Jossey-Bass.

7 Hackman, R. J. (2002), *Leading Teams: Setting the Stage for Great Performances*. Boston, MA: Harvard Business School Press.

8 Hackman, R. J. (2002), *Leading Teams: Setting the Stage for Great Performances*. Boston, MA: Harvard Business School Press.

9 Pentland, A. (2012), 'The New Science of Building Great Teams'. *Harvard Business Review*. Available from: https://hbr.org/2012/04/the-new-science-of-building-great-teams (Accessed 2 December 2016).

10 Katzenbach, J. R. and Smith, D. K. (1993), *The Wisdom of Teams: Creating the High-Performance Organization*. Boston, MA: Harvard Business School Press.

11 Hackman, R. J. (2002), *Leading Teams: Setting the Stage for Great Performances*. Boston, MA: Harvard Business School Press.

12 Deloitte (2016), *Global Human Capital Trends 2016. The New Organisation: Different by Design.* Texas: Deloitte University Press.

13 Goleman, D., Boyatzis, R. and McKee, A. (2002), *Primal Leadership: Learning to Lead with Emotional Intelligence.* Boston, MA: Harvard Business School Press.

14 Fiedler, F. E. (1958), *Leader Attitudes and Group Effectiveness.* Urbana: University of Illinois Press.

15 Janis, I. (1972), *Victims of Groupthink: A Psychological Study of Foreign-policy Decisions and Fiascoes.* Boston, MA: Houghton Mifflin.

16 Edmondson, A. C. (2010), *Teaming: How Organizations Learn, Innovate, and Compete in the Knowledge Economy.* San Francisco: Jossey-Bass.

17 Weick, K. E. (2002), 'Leadership When Events Don't Play by the Rules'. *Reflections: The SoL Journal*, 4(1), 30–2.

18 Stern, E. (2015), 'From Warning to Sense-Making: Understanding, Identifying and Responding to Strategic Crises'. *OECD.*

19 Kahneman, D. (2011), *Thinking Fast and Slow.* London: Penguin Books.

20 Collins, J. (2001), *Good to Great: Why Some Companies Make the Leap and Others Don't.* London: Random House Business Books.

21 Kline, N. (1999), *Time to Think: Listening to Ignite the Human Mind.* London: Octopus Books.

Chapter 6

1 In my experience, the concepts of *brand* and *reputation* are used without discipline and interchangeably. That's understandable. They share many attributes. Both are emotional and intangible and are about an expectation of performance and are about a relationship an organization has with its stakeholders. Critically, therefore both are about trust. However, my preference is to join Richard Ettenson and Jonathan Knowles, in their 2008 opinion piece *Don't Confuse Reputation with Brand* for MIT Sloan Management Review, which is to consider *brand* as being a construct that is orientated around *customers* whereas *reputation* is orientated around all those wider stakeholders who, together and in conjunction with customers, give an organization its *(social) licence to operate.* This includes employees, regulators, governments, shareholders etc. It's not the 'right' answer. But, it is in my view a helpful way to consider the two concepts.

2 Stern, K. (2016), 'Maybe the Right-wing media isn't crazy after all'. *Vanity fair.* Available from: http://www.vanityfair.com

3 Regester, M., and Larkin, J. (2008), *Risk, Issues and Crisis Management in Public Relations*, 4th edn. London: Kogan Page.

4 Fink, S. (2002), *Crisis Management: Planning for the Inevitable.* Lincoln: iUniverse, Inc.

5 Bull, P. (2003), *The Microanalysis of Political Communication*. London: Routledge.

6 Regester, M. and Larkin, J. (2005), *Risk, Issues and Crisis Management,* 3rd edn. London: Kogan Page.

7 Leith, S. (2011), *You Talkin' To Me?: Rhetoric from Aristotle to Obama*. London: Profile Books.

8 Paxman, J. (2002), *The Political Animal: An Anatomy*. London: Penguin Books.

9 The only difference to this is when undertaking what is referred to as a 'down-the-line' interview. This involves looking directly into the camera as the interviewer poses questions via an earpiece. In this case, it is necessary to try and imagine the camera as a face, look at the point in which the 'eyes' might be (one-third down the barrel of the camera) and keep your eyes fixed there. No matter what distraction and no matter how hard the question put to you is.

Chapter 7

1 Carlyle, T. (1841), *On Heroes, Hero-Worship and the Heroic in History*. London: James Fraser.

2 Hersey, P. and Blanchard, K. H. (1969), *Management of Organizational Behavior – Utilizing Human Resources*. New Jersey/Prentice Hall.

3 Allison, S. T. and Goethals, G. R. (2014), '"Now he belongs to the ages": The heroic leadership dynamic and deep narratives of greatness', in *Conceptions of Leadership: Enduring Ideas and Emerging Insights*. New York: Palgrave Macmillan, pp. 167–183.

4 Rajah, R. and Arvey, R. D. (2013), 'Helping group members develop resilience'. In DuBrin, A. J. (ed.), *Handbook of Research on Crisis Leadership in Organizations*. Cheltenham: Edward Elgar Publishing Ltd.

5 American Psychological Association (2016), 'The Road to Resilience'. *APA*. Available from: http://www.apa.org/helpcenter/road-resilience.aspx (Accessed 21 December 2016).

6 Richardson, G. E. (2002), 'The metatheory of resilience and resiliency'. *Journal of Clinical Psychology,* 58(3), 307–21.

7 HeavyRunner, I. and Marshall, K. (2003), 'Miracle survivors: Promoting resilience in Indian students'. *Tribal College Journal*, 14(4), 14–18.

8 Richardson, G. E. (2002), 'The metatheory of resilience and resiliency'. *Journal of Clinical Psychology,* 58(3), 307–21.

9 In the years following the development of the contingency theories, two theoretical concepts emerged in the field of leadership. The first was *transactional* leadership theory which emerged during the 1970s and which is typically associated with the leader's ability to find suitable reward for the follower to encourage the follower to undertake his or her request. The second, which emerged around the same time, is *transformational leadership* which requires the leader to convince followers to look beyond self-interest to see and reach towards a common good. It is typically associated with *charismatic leadership* which I have touched on briefly earlier in the chapter.

Chapter 8

1 Fink, S. (2002), *Crisis Management: Planning for the Inevitable*. Lincoln: iUniverse, Inc.

2 Wooten, L. P. and James, E. H. (2008), 'Linking Crisis Management and Leadership Competencies: The Role of Human Resource Development'. *Advances in Developing Human Resources*, 10 (3), 352–79.

3 Fink, S. (2002), *Crisis Management: Planning for the Inevitable*. Lincoln: iUniverse, Inc.

4 Maslow, A. H. (1943), 'A Theory of Human Motivation'. *Psychological Review* 50, 370–96.

5 Roux-Dufort, C. (2000), 'Why Organizations Don't Learn from Crises: The Perverse Power of Normalization'. *Review of Business*, 21 (3), 25–30.

6 Taleb, N. N. (2012), *Antifragile: Things that Gain from Disorder*. New York: Random House.

Chapter 9

1 Palin, A. (22 January 2016), 'Where did FT500 chief executives go to business school?'. The Financial Times. Available from: https://www.ft.com (accessed 03 March 2017).

2 Bennis, W. G. and O' Toole, J. (2005), 'How Business schools lost their way'. *Harvard Business Review*. Available from: https://hbr.org (accessed 07 July 2017).

3 Bennis, W. (2012), 'Have Business Schools Found Their Way?'. *Bloomberg*. Available from: https://www.bloomberg.com/ (accessed 03 March 2017).

4 Academy of Management. 'How can Business Schools Develop Leaders?'. *Academy of Management*. Available from: http://aom.org/ (accessed 03 March 2017).

5 De Cremer, D. (23 January 2012), 'Leaders need a lesson in crisis management: An awareness of how failure develops should be a part of the business school curricula'. *The Financial Times*. Available from: https://www.ft.com (accessed 03 March 2017).

INDEX